S0-AEX-083

BOOKS BY PAUL GALLICO

Farewell to Sport
Adventures of Hiram Holliday
The Secret Front
The Snow Goose
Lou Gehrig—Pride of the Yankees
Golf Is a Nice Friendly Game
Confessions of a Story Writer
The Lonely
The Abandoned
Trial By Terror
The Small Miracle
The Foolish Immortals
Snowflake
Love of Seven Dolls
Thomasina
The Steadfast Man
Mrs. 'Arris Goes to Paris
Ludmila
Too Many Ghosts
Mrs. 'Arris Goes to New York
The Hurricane Story
Further Confessions of a Story Writer
Scruffy
Coronation
Love, Let Me Not Hunger
The Day the Guinea Pig Talked
The Hand of Mary Constable
The Day Jean Pierre was Pignapped
Mrs. 'Arris Goes to Parliament
The Golden People

THE GOLDEN PEOPLE

This unique remembrance from the days of yore includes five of the Golden People in one photograph, as they appeared at a World's Champions Dinner sponsored by the Madison Square Garden Club. Top row: Babe Ruth, Gene Tunney, Johnny Weissmuller. Front row seated: Bill Tilden and Bob Jones. On the end standing is Bill Cook, the greatest hockey player of those days, and seated next to Jones, Fred Spencer and Charlie Winters, the championship six-day bike race team.

THE
GOLDEN PEOPLE

by Paul Gallico

DOUBLEDAY & COMPANY, INC., GARDEN CITY, N. Y.

1965

Library of Congress Catalog Card Number 65-19889
Copyright © 1964, 1965 by Paul Gallico

First Edition. Printed in the United States of America

TO DON MAXWELL

Whose Idea It Was

Contents

To the generation unborn when I was sports editor of the tabloid New York *Daily News*, let me introduce myself as an ex-sportswriter who, from 1923 through 1936, wrote a seven-day-a-week, thousand-word sports column and traveled the length and breadth of the United States, reporting games and their players.

Between times, for the sake of inside stories, one hobnobbed with famous athletes, played golf with them, looked in upon their private lives, admired or denounced them, and lived with them through a period we called "The Golden Decade" and which my colleague, Westbrook Pegler, named "The Era of Wonderful Nonsense."

It was both of these, that ten years between 1920 and 1930 and even beyond, with its first million-dollar prizefights and the adulation of sports heroes to the point almost of national hysteria.

Peace had broken out after World War I, bringing an expanding economy, a booming stock market, and not a cloud anywhere upon the horizon. Rockets were only for the Fourth of July; the split atom was no more than a physicist's dream. We had succeeded in making the world safe for democracy. Kaiser Bill was on the dust heap and no foreign power was menacing us. We were like children let out of school. All this was close to half a century ago.

There can be nothing quite so irritating to a new generation than a member of an earlier one mumbling into his beard about the super heroes he knew in his day. When I was a young sports-writer I had both read and listened to the old-timers going on about the greats of their era, and I vowed that when I reached that stage I would never do the same.

I have now found the breaking of this vow a most enjoyable experience. To begin with, it was a silly one to make and must be ascribed to the hot intolerance of youth. Experience teaches that every succession must look with a kindly eye and expanding imagination, backward upon the heroes of its day. So it has al-ways been. So it must always be. Who was I to attempt to inter-rupt this chain?

But it is not my intention to insist that the Golden People I wrote about and the athletes I covered in that decade and a half were the greatest ever, but only to tell you something of what they were like viewed now in long retrospect; how we re-garded them and what they meant to us during the times when they flourished.

A writer, no matter what lofty attitude he may assume, in the final analysis writes to earn a living. But often the subject matter he chooses, and the manner in which he presents it, is done for his own pleasure and escape from the ever-haunting problems that dog us all.

From time to time to his surprise, he finds that what has suc-ceeded in amusing and diverting him, has also managed to do the same for his readers.

The essays which appear in this book in greatly expanded form were written originally for the Chicago *Tribune* and the *Daily News* and syndicated in newspapers throughout the United States, and my enjoyment in renewing my memories of athletes I once admired and respected found a sympathetic echo among readers.

Hence, then, this collection as a memento to other times, other customs, other heroes.

PAUL GALLICO

Monaco, September 21, 1964

Illustrations

CHAPTER 1

The Mirror

It would appear that not only deeds but time endows names with a particular magic.

When I was this callow, young man growing up in New York in the early 1900s, I was fascinated, of course, by great names in sports that passed before my eyes or filled my ears. One read or heard about John L. Sullivan, James J. Corbett, Bob Fitzsimmons, Jim Jeffries, Sam Langford, Battling Nelson, Stanley Ketchel, Joe Gans, Terry McGovern, and Abe Attell from the prize ring; Christy Mathewson, Honus Wagner, Napoleon Lajoie, Willie Keeler, Eddie Plank, Ed Walsh, Big Chief Bender, and many more in baseball. I never saw these men perform, for by the time I became a sportswriter in 1922 their courses were run and they had vanished from the scene. But they were contemporary with my childhood and their names rang like the striking of brazen bells.

Yet, when I was grown they belonged already to the past and it was the old ones who were still recalling them as they had seen them in their prime. These names had filled the minds and hearts of a whole era of sports-loving men who wished to remember them even though they had left the stage and were no more to be seen.

It would seem that human beings have several alter egos and that we are able to live many lives, particularly if our own happens to be humdrum or we are so fortunate as to be endowed with imagination. Ever since the later American Republic took shape with comparative peace and prosperity coming to it after the Civil War and we began to look and behave like a nation, sports have provided the major share of this vicarious existence.

We might picture ourselves as leaders of men, captains of industry, generals, admirals, soldiers of fortune, spellbinders, Presidents, all of the great archetypes of history. But for almost a hundred years, close and warmest to the American heart has been the image of ourselves on the pitching mound, holding the fate of the game in the hollow of our glove, or equally menacing at the plate, waving the big bat about to explode the bases-loaded game and Series-winning home run.

With the savagery of pioneering days only a generation or two away, we could see ourselves, too, in that triumphant figure of the early prize ring, the red, white, and blue woven into the belt of our trunks, fists balled into fighting gloves, standing over a fallen foe while the count tolled to ten, the thousands cheering and sweeping us from the ring upon their shoulders.

There were football players, too, with stirring names: Jim Thorpe of Carlisle, Walter Eckersall of Chicago, Frank Hinkey and Pudge Heffelfinger of Yale, Edgar Allen Poe of Princeton from the days when only men from Harvard, Princeton, Yale, Pennsylvania, and occasionally Army made up the All-American team.

Baseball, football, boxing; three rough, dangerous, bruising contact sports were the favorites of the times which themselves had been rough, bruising, and brutal. In the early days of the nation, you had to be a man to survive and fight your way to the top.

Because of its very toughness, during that era just preceding the turn of the century and through it as well, there was something slightly disreputable about professional sports which surely made them all the more attractive to growing-up youngsters. Somehow games and players could not seem to avoid being connected with that wondrous oasis of sin, the corner saloon, where a large part of American low-caste life was lived.

Matches were made in those saloons, bets offered and taken, the skill, the records, and the achievements of athletes were priority barroom talk. The athletes of the day were not only powerful, heavy-muscled men and roaring extroverts, but two-fisted drinkers as well. Beer and whiskey were the tipple and drunkenness far from uncommon, often on the field or in the ring. Even

the college football players in their moleskins, with no more protection than a headband for their thick skulls, were notorious
hefters of the beer stein. In those days it was considered good
for you. And an echo of it carried over even to my day when
Jim Rice, the Columbia crew coach, kept a barrel of ale in the
boathouse, and after each day's workout we lined up with our
mugs for our ration "to take the edge off."

Boxing *was* disreputable, frequently outlawed, and had to be
conducted in secret places, in hiding from the police. Baseball
players were hardboiled, tobacco-chewing, brawling ruffians
themselves, almost on a par with prize fighters and certainly not
socially acceptable. In addition to sports *per se* there developed
a character in those times who was known as a "Sport." A Sport
was one who patronized prize fighting, baseball, horse racing,
and cock fighting. His home away from home was that same
corner saloon and he was hell on seducing servant girls as well.
For relaxation he went to Coney Island.

The Sport has disappeared from the scene, just as have the
old-time bruisers, battlers, and roughneck ballplayers, the corner
saloon, the barroom prize ring, the flying wedge on the football
field, the handlebar mustache and the bowler hat, the straw
katy, the prewar bartender, and the free lunch counter.

The sports of those days, the athletes, the manner in which
the participants as well as the spectators conducted themselves,
were a reflection of the times and the people. When the great
names had had their day, when the passing years had turned
them into graybeards, the era was over.

But this must be remembered. The one thing which every
athlete has had in common with past, present, and future genera-
tions, ever since man has had the leisure to take part in sports
either actively or vicariously, is that he reflects the age in which
he lives. He is a far more visible part of those times than almost
any other feature. By them we are able clearly to see and judge
ourselves.

We learn almost as much about the ancients from their sports
as we do from their history. The Greeks were a nation of poets
and artists, of great lovers of beauty. They ran foot races, leaped,
hurdled, wrestled, sent the discus arching through the air, competed in music, singing, and the dance.

The Romans were just the opposite, hard-nosed, brutal, aggressive. Their sport was death; their entertainment maiming and killing. Their contests were battles. There were no winners and losers, but only survivors. Their games described them and their times to a "t."

Jousting was a sport indicative of its era and those who took part in it. And a contest it was, even though it was training and preparation for warfare and combat. For if you will look into the archives of the College of Heralds in London—those heralds who were the arbiters, directors, and umpires of these dangerous diversions—you will find records of some of the medieval sporting afternoons, complete with an actual box score that cannot be understood or interpreted today, any more than archaeologists thousands of years from now, digging at the site of New York City, will be able to make out what: "AB. R. H. TB. PO. A. E." and the strings of figures beneath meant to baseball.

With the coming of gunpowder and the art of killing at a distance, pastimes ceased having a military background. Fencing remained a hangover from the necessity of handling a sword. The French invented one of the first wall games, *jeu de paume,* which later developed into court tennis and finally, lawn tennis as we know it, as well as handball. The Scots began whacking a feathered ball with a crooked stick and golf was born. The dandies of Regency England enjoyed the refined cruelties of bare-knuckle prize fighting, steeplechasing, fox hunting, and the bloody tatters of the cock pit.

But for the most part the sports, pastimes, and recreations during man's brief period of noted or remembered history is shrouded in darkness. The actual time of recorded sport is so short that it is, in fact, no more than a wink of an eye in the saga of modern man. There is a threefold reason for this: From the Middle Ages to our era, sports was (1) unimportant, (2) there were no sportswriters to report on whatever games there were (always excepting our heralds scoring the tilts), and (3) there were no journals to print what they might have written.

Nevertheless, even in that miniscule passage of reported events in sport, the decade of 1920–30 stands out as the most remarkable of the entire period and remains so to this day.

Yet almost all of the records made in that decade have already been smashed. Superb performers in every sport have emerged since; there has been no falling off of colorful and extraordinary characters. Despite this, the Golden People of the Golden Decade are still outstanding, not only for their accomplishments, but for the mirror they held up to their times. The nation was yet innocent and naïve and only beginning to acquire those unhappy attributes of cynicism and sophistication that are the concomitants of maturity. As we have grown up, so we have grown away from some of the delicious idiocies and passionate devotion to sports and sportsmen which were part and parcel of the Golden Decade.

There were a number of major features characterizing this period which can never happen again in exactly that way, for the simple reason that they were firsts. Sports were suddenly inundated with money and publicity and blossomed into social acceptance.

For the first time professional games participants played themselves into the millionaire class and athletes of every kind achieved more wealth than ever could have been dreamed of by the toughians who moiled and toiled when I was a boy.

For the first time male and female athletes were given publicity, newspaper reportage, and space usually reserved for the doings of crowned heads, major natural disasters, and wars.

The decade marked the rise into the domain of public excitement of three sports heretofore restricted to the wealthy: golf, tennis, and polo. Prior to this time there were only two names that stand out in my memory—Francis Ouimet in golf and Maurice McLoughlin in tennis. In 1913 Ouimet, the first amateur ever to win a U. S. Open golf championship, defeated two tough old pros, Harry Vardon and Ted Ray. And in the years 1912 and 1913, Maurice McLoughlin of California won the U.S. outdoor singles tennis championship with a hard-hitting, dynamic style of play which overnight turned lawn tennis from a sissy, ice-cream-pants, society diversion to an annual thriller. And polo produced a Tommy Hitchcock. Suddenly these neglected sports began to present an astonishing set of heroes and heroines as well as enormous box-office receipts.

This remarkable ten years further saw the most fabulous set

of champions arise in every game, amateur or professional, not only from the point of view of performance, but of character as well. Every one of them was a colorful extrovert of one kind or another. Each had a romance connected with him or her, and these legends themselves were reflections of our age of innocence, for they were all success stories, the great American fairy tale, the rise from rags to riches, the first such actually dramatized before our eyes.

The era alone would have to be set down as unique, since it was practically the last time we believed in anything or anyone, including the happy ending.

If the mirror that earlier sports held up to us hinted at a people barely emerging from infanthood, whose toilet training and table manners were not yet altogether secure, the athletes of that splendid decade showed us up as wide-eyed romantics who could be ballyhooed into believing anything as long as there were heaps and heaps of money connected with it, right conquering wrong and virtue triumphant.

Drama and literature just preceding that period gave some indication of our national gullibility and essential psychological simplicity. *Pollyanna* and *Peg o' My Heart* were just two of the opuses popular during that period. The easiest thing in the world was to live by symbols. The horned devil tempted, angels clad in white nightgowns sprouted snow-white wings, the villain had a black mustache and wore a top hat, the hero golden curls and his shirt open at the neck. There were good women or bad women and no in-betweeners. Once you were fallen in that league, you had fell. The poor were deserving, the rich were not. Youth was supposedly molded by the Bible, but it was actually Horatio Alger, Frank Merriwell, Jr., and the Rover Boys by whom we lived.

There is one vestige of this marvelous callowness that has come down to us today and survived in the Western. The good guys wear white stetsons, the bad guys black ones. That is how you can tell them from far off and no mistaking one for the other. And look out for the fellow with the too-small mustache!

The judgments of our era were almost that simple. White or black, good guys or bad guys and no grays wanted or tolerated.

But one of the most unique and astonishing phenomenons of

this period was that in the twinkling of an eye, and overnight, as it were, an athlete who had been loved and admired as a good guy could turn into a baddie to be booed, hissed, and reviled. You will see this happen again and again in the following essays, the stories of the Golden People of this fabulous decade.

How we were able to accomplish this transition was one of the more astonishing phenomena of this age. But accomplish it we did, not only toward individuals but entire teams as well. A prize fighter who entered the arena as it rocked with cheers for him at the outset of one contest might find himself almost blasted from the premises by the booing that greeted him for the next. In some subtle and often indiscernible manner between the two appearances, the public had stripped him of his halo and adorned him with hoofs, horns, and forked tail. Ball clubs that had won a pennant and a World Series with roaring acclamation in the fall, found themselves drawing flies the following spring and jeers when they took the field. But whichever way it went, the rooting interest was stronger, more lively and vital than it had ever been before.

And only now, gazing upon it from the perspective of forty-five years, does one begin to understand it. From 1923 to 1936 I was in the thick of it myself, loving it, fascinated, swept away, spinning a daily tale in the most florid and exciting prose that I could muster, part of the great ballyhoo, member of the great gullibles, swallower of my own bait. I belonged to that category of sportswriters known as the "Gee-Whizzers," an utter, innocent romantic myself, who even if he no longer gave entire credence to Santa Claus, was a sucker for the theology of the good guys and the bad guys.

Modern sport itself emerged from its original cocoon of disrespectability into the daylight of acceptance by every class, strata, and walk of life in America, young and old, rich and poor, cultured aristocrat or ignoramus. That area of life was like a perpetual adventure serial. And in those days and in those times, we drugged ourselves with such romantic chronicles. We had just emerged from a serious war and now wanted no more of reality but only escape therefrom into the realms of the fanciful. Sports and sports stories and sports characters who were almost magical in their performance provided much of that escape.

Not a day went by when your newspaper could not unfold some tale of heroism, derring-do, extraordinary skill, or last minute in-the-clutch rescue. There was such a choice of paladins to worship from football, baseball, boxing, tennis, golf, swimming, foot running, even wrestling, ice skating, hockey, and polo, not to mention the little monkeys who rode the winning race horses, that there was never a moment winter, summer, spring, or fall, when your interest flagged. Someone you either loved or hated was always in the news.

Two new forms of journalistic literature were introduced. One was the serialized life story of some recent demigod such as the pitcher of a no-hit game, or one-round knockout artist, and the other the literary athlete who, even before he had rinsed the sweat from his body in the showers, was supposed to have rushed to his typewriter and indited an intimate, inside, personal account of just how he had done it. Or, in the case of forthcoming battle, how he was going to do it.

This in turn brought into being a new kind of hack artist, the ghost writer, who augmented his normal salary as a sportswriter by providing the hokum which appeared under the bylines of the most famous athletes of the country. This ploy gave rise to the immortal remark of the late Don Skene, one of the wittiest of the sportswriters of our times, who upon entering the press box of a World Series late and seeing most of his colleagues engaged in pounding out stories under names of a dozen or so of the heroes who had just left the field, cried, "My God, it looks like a haunted house!"

In the years to come not dissimilar shenanigans on radio and television, when utter nincompoops were made out to have the wisdom and erudition of a whole gaggle of Einsteins, brought stern repercussions, indictments for crime, and thunderous cries for cleanup. But in my day nobody was in the least put out by this ghost writing fraud, and much of the hogwash turned out in this manner was accepted as gospel. It was amusingly axiomatic that if there was any real news or inside story connected with either an event or a play, or some dramatic instant of the game, one never learned about it under the athlete's by-line.

Flash and extra editions containing the results of an important prize fight sold hundreds of thousands more copies of a daily paper. Well-drilled, -trained, and -rehearsed teams in arena, editorial, and composing room collaborated in competing for the reduction of time by fractions of seconds from the instant when the defeated pug lay quivering on the canvas, oblivious of the fatal toll of ten, to the moment when the presses would start tolling and newsboys would seize the bundles to ring the night-time welkin with their cries. Expensive telephone wires were leased to bring the voice of the blow-by-blow reporter directly to the ear of the compositor at his linotype machine. Hospital ambulances were perverted to rush photographic plates from the scene of combat to the newspaper darkrooms downtown, bells clanging, defying red lights and traffic regulations as though delivering someone in mortal agony. Airplanes not being the reliable means of transportation they are today, and wirephoto transmission as yet in its infancy, solo locomotives were often engaged to bring pictures of sports events from out of town. One tried anything one could get away with to hit the street first and satisfy the average citizen's insatiable appetite for pictures and story of a contest.

I seem to be telling now of an era that appears more like a hundred than only thirty to forty years ago, so far are we from being the same people we were then, and what in those times was deadly earnest to us must seem utterly laughable today. We are different in every way, certainly wiser and undoubtedly sadder.

When this generation passes it will be the aging reporters looking back from the edge of the twenty-first century who, perhaps, will be able to tell us the kind of people we are this immediate day, from the manner in which we behaved vis-à-vis our athletes, their games, and their personalities and they toward us. In the meantime, here is my own look backward from the vantage point of 1965 down through the corridors of the years leading to 1920; what I remember and how it all looks to me today.

The Babe himself.

CHAPTER **2**

Babe Ruth

(1895–1948)

When first I blocked out this series and sat down to plan the inclusion of those I remembered with the greatest warmth and pleasure, men and women who had provided me with not only copy, but thrills and enjoyment over the years distilled from their personalities as well as from their prowess, the first name I put down was that of George Herman (Babe) Ruth.

He was Number One. No weighing-up, no shillyshallying comparisons. There he stood before me in belted camel's hair coat and cap, a friendly, sardonic grin spreading all over his ugly map and his rumbling laugh bubbling up from his vast interior. Although he had been dead for sixteen years, he was as alive and vital to me as in the days when I was traveling on the Yankee Special. I played handball with him in Jack O'Brien's gymnasium during the winter months. In the summer, from my eyrie in the press box, I watched and marveled as he boomed the ball over the walls of the stadia of New York, Washington, Boston, Detroit, and other arenas of the American League circuit, to be retrieved by some urchin far out on Railroad Avenue and kept by him forever as an object of veneration. Once more I felt the curious thrill of affection this man engendered in all of us who were associated with him and who were his Boswells.

Looking backward, I see the figure of Ruth during his years with the Yankees far from being paled by the passage of time. On the contrary, for me the light he once shed if anything burns still more brightly. He was Gargantua in human form. No one has appeared upon the scene since his death to match him or give us any cause either to diminish or forget him.

The Reform School kid from Baltim

"There she goes!"

During the baseball season from April to the World Series at
the beginning of October, and often a good part of the winter
months as well, the Babe lived with us daily and we with him
until he became a better-known and better-publicized figure even
than the President of the United States. He could not have
achieved this had he not been worthy of it, had he not been the
extraordinary figure he was with the capacity to make men, small
boys, and even women love and care about him.

It has been said that people like Ruth, Dempsey, Tunney, Tilden, and all the sensational champions of the era, were made by
newspaper ballyhoo, the opening up of newspaper columns and
the increasing number of sports pages. But this is not so. Looking
back upon the turmoil and the hubbub from the vantage of retrospect there is no doubt in my mind which came first, the chicken
or the egg.

It was the characters that made people care deeply. The newspapers discovered that caring meant circulation, which brought
advertising and advertising a share of the rich, ripe melon we
were cutting up in our postwar spree.

WIDE WORLD

The great Ruthian whiff.

In times past we had been interested in and excited by prize fighters and baseball players, but we had never been so individually involved or joined in such a mass outpouring of affection as we did for Ruth.

It seemed as though after the war we looked upon almost everything and everyone in sports with quite different eyes than we did at the century's turn. There was, of course, the usual postwar population explosion, but more than this, we felt we had earned the right to substitute the gaiety and thrill of sports combat for the real thing that we wanted to forget.

Editors were supposed to be sensitive to the public pulse. They were indeed. They opened up the pages to this different kind of hero or heroine, and into this newly created vacuum strode the giants. The newspapers that followed their careers most closely were rewarded with soaring sales and circulation figures. The big, black headline, as strident as those reporting any form of battle action, "BABE HITS NOS. 32 & 33," rolled from the presses and came out as gold and silver.

If the Babe had not been the Babe, the man, the character, the personality he was, he might have passed merely as an exceptional hitter.

It was the caring about him that counted.

During that resplendent decade and a little beyond, Babe Ruth compiled his fabulous record of 714 home runs in his lifetime; 60 in one season; 11 seasons of more than 40 home runs, as well as a lifetime collection of 2056 bases on balls and 1330 strikeouts, and at the same time became a living legend and the best-known, most loved baseball player of all time.

This is to take nothing from your Roger Maris, who hit 61 home runs in 162 games, a remarkable feat indicative of a fine athlete and a splendid batter.

Yet there is one great difference between the extravagant sets of home runs hit by Babe Ruth and Roger Maris. For the latter was a pursuit, an attempt to surpass which produced some stirring tensions, but the way led through known territory. Someone had been there before and established the fact that it was possible. The home runs amassed by Babe Ruth, and in particular his great record of 60 in 154 games, was the sheerest pioneering and exploration into the uncharted wildernesses of sport. There was something almost of the supernatural and the miraculous connected with him, too. And this in turn had much to do with us, the ebullience of our times, the exuberance and the joy of living. Our music, literature, and drama reflected this light-hearted pleasure and so did the ceaseless click of the hits off the bat of the Babe, a kind of metronome to our success.

The Babe was a bundle of paradoxes. Somehow one of the most appealing things about him was that he was neither built, nor did he look like an athlete. He did not even look like a ballplayer. Although he stood six feet two inches and weighed 220 pounds, his body was pear-shaped and even when in tip-top condition he had a bit of a belly. His barrel always seemed too much for his legs, which tapered into a pair of ankles as slender almost as those of a girl. The great head perched upon a pair of round and unathletic shoulders, presented a moon of a face, the feature of which was the flaring nostrils of a nose that was rather like a snout. His voice was deep and hoarse, his speech crude and earthy, his ever-ready laughter a great, rumbling gurgle that arose from the caverns of his middle. He had an eye that was abnormally quick, nerves and muscular reactions to match, a supple wrist, a murderous swing, and a gorgeously truculent, competitive spirit.

Maris, for instance, must be similarly endowed strength- and reactionwise, but they say that Roger is a cold fish and nothing rides his long ball but power. There was always an emotion of some kind accompanying the Babe's home run hit as it departed from the premises. No ballplayer to my knowledge or recollection, with the possible exception of Willie Mays, ever delivered the goods with such infectious gusto, or more greatly enjoyed his abilities and his successes. Life for the Babe consisted of women, food, liquor, and baseball, and when his appetites for the first three were appeased, there was nothing that gave him more intense satisfaction than whipping the ball out of the playing field, and no one ever put more effort into the attempt.

This love of and delight in accomplishment spread to the spectators in the stands. His rooters savored his triumphs vicariously;

his enemies reveled in his failures. For his misses were as prodigious as his hits. At the end of a swung strike his legs would
be braided like a barroom pretzel, and he would be facing three-
quarters of the compass around from where he had started.

It was the unique capacity of the Babe's warm, extravagant,
vital personality which enabled the onlookers to play the game
with him, to share his feelings, his fervor, and above all his implacable intent as, standing over the plate, he peered out toward
the mound and menaced the pitcher with a preliminary wave or
two of his bat. At that moment in a packed Yankee Stadium we
all became one with him, 70,000 Ruths of us on the big days,
equipped with the determination and extraordinary power to
wreck the ball game. There took place a transference in which the
least and humblest nobody in the stands found himself swelling
with the magnificent afflatus of the Babe.

It was our decade that Ruth was expressing, the golden touch,
the can't-be-beaten, the we-can-do-it, the key to success and
wealth, money in the pocket and two chickens in every pot.

He could pitch too.

Application of power.

When the famous, dry "click" was heard as the white ball arched
and fielders stood with their hands helplessly placed upon their
hips, their heads turned for a last farewell glimpse of the departing sphere, the great roar that exploded from the stands was for
the Babe, but the salute was also to the unconquerable, unquenchable us. We had done it again.

You might think, perhaps, that this plethora of home runs
would cheapen them and satiate our appetites. Far from it; every
time Ruth came to bat he was on his way to some kind of record.
Every ball he expelled from the stadia was one more link in the
chain of continuing and progressing miracles. The impossible was
becoming the probable, and for the price of admission would take
place before one's very eyes. And the Babe's utter demolishing
of every prior home run record was just another verification of
the opulence of our times.

The home run, then, during the rule of Ruth became in a way the equivalent of the jackpot. It disgorged runs in showers and the arch-Croesus of this largess was the weird-looking man with the barrel body, spindly legs, and pudding face. For though the denigrators will talk about the advent of the rabbit ball and the explosive center, the fact remains that during the early days of the decade when Ruth was already racking up forty or more home runs, nobody else was hitting them—certainly not that many, until the coming of Lou Gehrig. Home runs flowed from his bat the way gold was supposed to pour from the cornucopia of the Goddess of Plenty.

Baseball, of course, is a team game: nine men acting in concert to expunge the batter; batters collaborating their efforts in succession to throw the defense out of gear, put runners on base, advance them, and turn them into runs. But Ruth additionally always had a private duel with the pitcher. In fact most of the great man's effort was concentrated upon an unaided performance. If he connected, he needed no further assistance to get him around the bases. Any player who had the good fortune to be on ahead of him, came home automatically as the Babe dog-trotted around the bases, doffing his cap. With rare exceptions his home runs were such complete affairs that there was no call for speed, or even the semblance of running.

The game, as you know, is so constituted that a runner who lags on the bases may be tagged out by a member of the opposing team, if he has the ball in his hands. But after Ruth had applied his magic bat to a missile, there simply was no more ball with which to tag anyone. It was either in the pocket of some delirious fan in the right-field bleachers, or rolling along in the gutter of a thoroughfare outside the ball park. A new one had to be produced before the game could continue. Ruth conceded touching the bases as he jogged around them, in the manner of royalty acknowledging ancient protocol or formality.

This left the combat area largely up to Ruth at the plate with the opposing pitcher on the mound. And never before had the spectators at ball games and all those who attended them vicariously through their newspapers or their just-budding radio sets, become quite so aware of the nature of the struggle between the thrower and the hitter.

The man on the mound had a bag of tricks at his disposal. He could throw the ball with blinding speed, or float it deceptively. He could make it swoop, yaw, drop, sail, or, soaped with saliva, break maniacally before the plate in a manner that no man could foresee.

Against this highly scientific hocus-pocus of imparting spin and unorthodox behavior to a ball in flight, the batter had to respond with a camera-lens eye and photo-flash reaction.

Now none of this is news to the baseball fan, nor is it intended to be. It is only to remind him of the extent to which the situation of George Herman Ruth at bat and any one of a hundred pitchers on the mound, became such a personal affair. The Babe was not interested in being presented with four balls and a walk. He was not looking to bloop a single into short center, or even drive a double between two outfielders. His sole ambition was to lace that ball out of the park and, singlehandedly, contribute from one to four runs at a time. The pitcher's aim and desire was to prevent this, to force him into three prodigious whiffies, or to slide the third one across between shoulder and knees with the big bat still on the Babe's shoulders. Let it be said here and now that the pitcher's problem was further complicated by the fact that prior to this time, none of them had ever encountered so dangerous and miraculous a hitter. It undoubtedly worked upon their nerves. It was unfair to bring magic into baseball. In a way it was something like fighting against the man who wielded the sword named "Excalibur." It gave him an edge.

And this was something new in sports, wholly and utterly novel, never before seen on any baseball diamond; something akin to the unstoppable force meeting the immovable object. For the first time in the not-too-long history of the game, the pitcher was throwing to a man who was capable of breaking up the ball game at any moment. Day in and day out we watched these duels with unflagging excitement and exaltation and all of America watched too. At the hour of Evensong the question would arise upon millions and millions of lips, "Did the Babe hit one today?"

Ruth had a fine, ruffianly sense of humor. He was able to laugh at himself, particularly after a prodigious strikeout. But there was no laughter that became him better than the rumbling gurgle of satisfaction following upon that brief explosion, signalizing the fact that the opposition had guessed wrong and he had guessed right.

The Ruthian humor was not restricted only to the demolishment of the pride of the man on the mound, it went further than that. It must be remembered that the pitcher, while it is his strength and skill that speeds the ball, collaborates with the catcher, who calls by secret sign for the kind of delivery he thinks will do the trick. This catcher, also by signal, is frequently in communication with the Great Brain, the manager on the bench.

The Babe happily thought, and often spoke, aided by the four-letter word. When he connected and the ball hissed its farewell in the sky as he trotted around the base paths, the Babe was supremely and ecstatically content in the fact that he had given a four-letter wording to all three, pitcher, catcher, manager. This joy was so visibly effulgent and effervescent, the four-letter word was so evidently hovering about his head or shimmering over the field as he toured the bases, even though his lips might not be moving, that it was communicated to us in an exquisite and re-laxing catharsis. Some part of this wonderful feeling spread to every corner of the United States.

There was something else that helped to make for the enor-mous, vicarious enjoyment the masses derived out of Babe Ruth's performances on and off the diamond. For not only did he not look like an athlete, neither did he behave like one. There had been big leaguers before and will have been since, who suffered from too great an attraction to the bottle, the flesh, or the dinner table, but never one who so heartily indulged in and relished all three as Babe Ruth.

Thus he became the beloved alter ego of every man who wished himself able to stuff, drink, wench, and still come through. Ruth could and did. He broke every training rule and regulation that ever was included in *mens sano corpore sane* and still pulled those booming, luscious, satisfying home runs off his bat, made impossible catches in the field, and threw strikes into the catcher's mitt to cut off runs at the plate with his bottom backed into the right-field wall.

A glimpse into baseball records will fill you in on the staggering "firsts" and "mosts" of the lifetime averages of the Babe in a career that stretched from 1914 to 1935. One could dizzy you with figures, but looking backward I find now, as then, that I am still far more interested in what this man meant to us and the strange love we all felt for him.

For this affection was not confined only to baseball fans or spectators. He was loved by millions of Americans who had never seen him play or, for that matter, even attended a ball game. Somehow Ruth had come to be regarded as a member of everyone's family, and we were concerned with his troubles and his problems as well as his successes, as though he was one of our own children. Like a child he was frequently naughty. The whole of the United States shared in his public punishments. When he was ill we all suffered with and for him and watched by his hospital bedside. When he was fined and suspended for insubordination and breaking training, we shuddered and sympathized. And there was that fantastic day in Chicago, when Root of the Cubs had two strikes on him and the Babe called his shot by pointing to the flagpole in center field and then hit the next pitch to the very same spot for a home run. Not only the World Series crowd and those of us in the press box, but practically every home in America thrilled as though the feat had been accomplished by our own son.

The Babe lived—well and heartily. He seemed to be filled with a mischievous joy and appreciation of all of the good things in life, and surely it was this great zest and enthusiasm which enabled Ruth to give so prodigiously when playing his game. His impish streak was at the bottom of the delight he took in the discomfiture of every pitcher who had thrown him a home run ball.

No doubt his antecedents and his rise, again an example of the great American success story, helped to inspire the outpourings of love from the masses of his admirers. For a poor and intractable

The magic of Ruth.

boy who had spent the greater part of his youth in a reform school for incorrigibles, he had come a long way and had earned the particular doting worship of gamins who, invariably, wherever he appeared, furnished the tail to his meteor-like presence. He had a feeling for children and consented genially to be their god. He was the hero of the millions like himself who were poor, neglected, and unsung, the messiah of the underprivileged and wretched young, and every time he went to bat he delivered an unmistakable sermon, "Ye, too, may enter into the Kingdom of Swat."

A baseball autographed by him became a unique and venerable object to be enshrined in the home. For a small boy to meet or touch him was to be suffused with the radiance and the glory, and the Babe even became endowed with powers of healing. If anyone should be looking to canonize a saint of baseball there are authentic records, all during our times, of Ruth saving the life of this or that sick child by a hospital bedside visit and the promise to hit a home run especially for him, and one which he always managed to keep.*

The sympathetic magic of the Babe extended even to the spectator in the stands. For after seeing a Ruthian homer one came away with a kind of ineffable glow in one's middle, and for a long time afterward had the feeling of something wonderful having happened that day.

Has there been a ballplayer since his era who has had such a grip upon the affection of the nation? I would think no. Not only has no such extraordinary figure appeared upon the sports scene, but our times and we, too, as people, have changed. Casting backward to the innocence of the decade between 1920 and 1930, we know now that our world of today has turned savage, cruel, and inhospitable. We are menaced from within and without and beset with fears, worries, and situations we have never had to face before. We have lost some of that capacity to care deeply about anyone or anything besides our immediate families. The fact that once there was an easier age, that there was such a man as Ruth when we were young and that he so endeared himself to us was really what was good about those old days.

---

* As a matter of fact, many years later I did canonize him in a short story called "Saint Bambino." I wrote this one sentimental evening some ten years after his death. As I remember it I had been listening to a World Series broadcast over the Armed Forces Network which reached me where I was living, isolated on a mountaintop in Liechtenstein. Suddenly I was aware of a great nostalgia for those times and for the Babe himself, and set to work. Sometimes fiction succeeds even better than fact on re-creating a character and bringing him to life. On the chance that I might have managed to accomplish this, the story is reproduced here as an Appendix to *The Golden People*.

"The simple, unassuming girl, daughter of a German-American family who owned a small delicatessen store on upper Amsterdam Avenue, New York City."

CHAPTER **3**

Gertrude Ederle

If you will look today into a modern almanac or record book, you will find under the heading of Channel Swimmers some two columns of names of men and women who have conquered this treacherous body of water under their own steam. Why they bothered to do so and still do, is anybody's guess. Even recently that much abused strait has been trampled and threshed by individuals determinedly trying to eke out firsts from its cross-currents, heavy tides, and choppy waters, including children and graybeards looking to be the youngest or the oldest or the fastest. Others have been attempting to swim it both ways in one gulp.

But up to the year 1926 there were only five who had made it; Matthew Webb of Britain, 1875; Thomas Burgess of Britain, who crossed in 1911; Henry F. Sullivan of the United States who, along with Enrique Tiraboschi of Argentina and Charles Toth, another American, swam it in 1923. Of these five the fastest time recorded was that of the Argentine, who swam from France to England in sixteen hours and thirty-three minutes. Many more had tried and failed, and those who succeeded were well-larded giants.

Women had attempted it in vain. The test of that particular body of water was thought to be too severe for the so-called weaker sex. This situation was corrected on August 6, 1926 when another name was added to this brief list. It was that of an eighteen-year-old girl, an American. She hustled from Cap Gris Nez to Dover in fourteen hours and thirty-one minutes, not only breaking the time record of the fastest man by two whole hours, but

achieving the only first that really mattered from then on. Her
name was Gertrude Ederle and she was the pioneer of her sex to
succeed in this arduous passage.

Females have been making the crossing ever since but the trips
are meaningless. Everest had been climbed, so to speak. It was
Gertrude Ederle who once and for all had softened the English
Channel for women and showed that it could be done.

That was thirty-nine years ago and nothing remains today but
that single line in the record books and the memory of the great
din unloosed in New York Harbor the day of her return from
abroad, when the whistle-cord of every steamship within range
was tied down. Sirens brayed and hooted as airplanes buzzed
and thundered overhead, pelting her with flowers as she stood
upon the deck of the city tug *Macom,* surrounded by municipal
dignitaries in plug hats and frock coats, who were escorting her
up the Bay.

In my ears still rings that great rolling roar which followed
her triumphant motorcade up Lower Broadway, swelling from
block to block as the crowd, packed from sidewalk to sidewalk,
caught its first glimpse of the young, brown-haired girl standing in
the back of an open car, her arms extended as though to em-
brace them all. In my mind's eye I can see this mass, so dense
that motorcycle police had to thrust open a lane for her passage
as the wildly enthusiastic welcomers rushed and fought for the
privilege of touching the car in which she rode. She progressed
through the canyons of the skyscrapers beneath the bizarre August snowfall of ticker tape, torn up telephone books, shredded
newspapers, broker's sheets and toilet rolls descending upon her
from every window.

For this paper blizzard was something new in the line of wel-
comes to returning heroes, which had developed since the war,
along with the incumbency as official City Greeter of the late
Grover Whalen, appointed to that stately office by New York's
Broadway playboy mayor, Jimmy Walker. Mr. Whalen was a
gorgeous piece of man, born to the top hat, striped trousers, frock
coat, and gardenia in the buttonhole which was his uniform when
he went down the Bay to receive an incoming celebrity. With his
pink face and black, toothbrush mustache, he was as much a part

Ederle the child, at the age of thirteen.

of the municipal scene as Battery Park, the Aquarium, and the downtown skyscrapers.

A routine had evolved in which the *Macom* chuffed down to Quarantine, the arriving V.I.P. was received officially by Mr. Whalen, transferred from the liner to the tug, and decanted at The Battery, where a cavalcade of open motorcars awaited. Then followed the ride up from Lower Broadway to City Hall, where his Honor the Mayor was enthroned to climax the reception.

Office workers in the tall buildings lining both sides of America's most famous street, having been alerted, waited like excited children with their home made storm. When the motorcade came past, they unloaded from the heights and the paper, fluttering down, was one of the prettiest sights you ever saw and strangely moving as well.

Spectators usually lined the sidewalks to watch the procession go by, but for Ederle the largest crowd ever turned out, spilling from the curbs and jamming the thoroughfare. Never before in the history of the city had there been such a demonstration for a sports hero; never before had the Department of Sanitation been called upon to sweep up so many tons of Broadway confetti. Not until the following year, when Lindbergh came back from France, were the decibels of cheers, tonnage of shredded paper, and hysterical warmth of welcome equaled or surpassed.

And all this for a simple, unassuming girl, the daughter of a German-American family who owned a small delicatessen store on upper Amsterdam Avenue in New York City.

This was the kind of welcome one would expect to be reserved for conquering admirals and generals, or crowned heads. But it was in this era that America produced a new royalty, the kings and queens of sport, as a vivid and thrilling demonstration of the workings of this unique democracy, where the poorest and the humblest could instantly become national heroes and heroines.

Gertrude Ederle, or Trudy as she was universally known both from affection as well as compact headlining, was one of these, and a shining example of the sudden magic that could envelop ordinary persons and overnight elevate them to fame and fortune.

One moment, as it were, she was an unknown, one of the

faceless millions inhabiting our teeming cities, a young girl who enjoyed the exercise of swimming competitions and the companionship of her clubmates, and the next she was a world celebrity.

And had she but understood the nature of the excitement, love, and admiration she had touched off, had she been less modest, simple, and unambitious, she too might have become a millionairess, a Queen Midas, turning everything she fingered to gold.

As it was, the day after the news of her courageous triumph over self and one of the world's most treacherous bodies of water had been broadcast, merchants, promotors, manufacturers, and motion picture and theatrical producers were lined up in the offices of her "managers." They were trying to thrust large sums of money upon them for endorsements of articles, personal appearances, engagements, and services of every kind connected with the gilded name of Ederle, which could be expected to bring an equally gilded return from the almost hysterical Ederle-loving American public. The child had, so to speak, done nothing that was either useful, good, or serviceable to humanity, and yet as far as we of that era were concerned, she had done everything and we were prepared to drown her, who had survived the Channel, in a flood of dollar bills.

The fact that most of these offers were fended off with some arrogance by a group of "managers" that suddenly mushroomed around this celebrity, was part of a personal tragedy that dogged Gertrude Ederle, but did not alter the fact that here was an attempt for the first time in the memory of man to bestow riches upon a swimmer.

The art itself had barely become a sport. Up to that time, practically, swimming was something one did at the beach in the summer, or when one fell into the water or capsized when sailing, to keep from drowning. What, then, was there suddenly about this, and particularly women's swimming, which saw it in this decade elevated to the very pinnacle of publicity?

For the answer one looks again at our times.

Still heavy-handed, hypocritical, censorious prudes, we had but recently emerged from the age of the long-stockinged, full-

The start—nervous tension and determination. Greased against the cold, Gertrude Ederle walks the sands of Cap Gris Nez to enter the Channel.

Triumph!

Swimmingly Yours
Gertrude Trudy Eder
NEW YORK
Successful Channel Sw
Aug. 6, 1926
Cap Gris Nez to Kingsdow

The battle. Fourteen miles off the French coast! Temptation, "Trudy, you must come out!" and the battle cry, "What for?"

skirted, bosom-swaddling bathing costume, the most ridiculous collection of woolen garments ever to conceal the female form divine. Men looked silly enough in their long drawers and half-sleeved, candy-striped, jersey tops, but it was the women dressed, apparently, more for going down into a mine than entering the sea, who really took the cake. One reason that swimming had failed to develop as a sport was simply that no one could move in the damn things. All they were good for was holding onto a rope and bobbing up and down in the Sea Bright, Sheepshead Bay, or Coney Island breakers. Any attempt at forward progress was soon brought to a halt by the drag of some twenty pounds of waterlogged clothing.

The revolutionary heroine who put an end to this nonsense

and freed women from this form of bondage was an Australian girl by the name of Annette Kellerman, a polio victim who took up swimming at the turn of the century as therapy for her crippled legs. It was Miss Kellerman who claimed that no woman had the brute strength to swim the English Channel, for she had made several attempts to do so herself and once had gotten three-quarters across before being forced to give up.

But it was not for this that her name became world-famous, but the fact that she introduced the first one-piece bathing suit for women. A spectacular exhibition swimmer, she went into vaudeville and motion pictures clad, or rather unclad, in this daring garment and girls, forever thereafter freed from the drag of shoes, stockings, bloomers, blouse, and hat, bought themselves "Annette Kellermans" and began to swim.

When I was a boy Annette Kellerman was a household word and I remember her, smooth and glistening as a seal, performing in a tank on the stage of the old Colonial Theatre on Broadway and 62nd Street, a house devoted to high-class vaudeville. The S.R.O. sign was out at the theater, and the balcony spotlights were reflected from many a bald pate. The sellout attendance had come ostensibly to see her doing the crawl, the backstroke, the jackknife, and the swan dives, but nobody at the box office was being kidded. The original Annette Kellerman bathing suit was still a slightly bulky affair of jersey wool, even though skirtless and sleeveless. Nevertheless, it made the question of how ladies were put together no longer a matter of vague speculation.

The tight-fitting, black silk racing suit was only a few years away, and women's swimming and diving competitions became a major attraction. Newspaper publishers discovered that whereas reproductions of nightclub cuties in leotards or tights might bar them from the mails, due to the Nice-Nellies in the post office censorship in Washington, photographs of an octet of naiads, lined up at the end of the pool in their wet, clinging, one-piece garments were legit, even though far more revealing.

An appreciable part of the great Florida real estate boom was built upon photographs of girl swimmers used in advertising, and certainly no newspaper ever suffered a drop in circulation when it was able to publish this kind of cheesecake. Even as late as 1932 the publisher of the *News*, Captain Joseph M. Patterson, one of the canniest newspapermen ever to give the public what it wanted, commanded me to instigate and organize a great swimming meet to be held in the public parks, and which I staged first in Central Park and later at Jones Beach, filling our pages for days with girls, girls, girls. And what girls!

Back in 1917, a scattering of young secretaries and career women had formed an organization known as the Women's Swimming Association around a nucleus of a small pool on the Lower East Side under the chaperonage of a remarkable woman, the late Charlotte Epstein, and coached by L. B. de Handley.

From this nucleus there exploded like fireworks the most astonishing and breathtaking collection of scintillating stars who were not only record-breaking championship swimmers and divers, but exquisitely lovely girls who became beauty queens and celebrities equal in fame almost to the reigning royalty of Hollywood. These included such unquestionable pippins as Aileen Riggin, Sybil Bauer, Martha Norelius, Helen Wainwright, Helen Meany, two sensational blondes named Georgia Coleman and Dorothy Poynton, Esther Williams, Josephine McKim and, of course, the one and only Eleanor Holm, the backstroke champion and one of the most beautiful nymphs ever seen in a bathing costume.

Gertrude Ederle, the daughter of the Amsterdam Avenue liverwurst purveyor, joined the Women's Swimming Association when she was thirteen and received all of her early teaching, coaching, and training there.

While Trudy was never a member of the W.S.A. beauty chorus, she was far from plain, and her somewhat Teutonic chubbiness, round, dimpled face, and fair-brown bobbed hair, were offset by agreeable features and an extraordinarily sweet expression.

She was of average height and not heavily muscled. Seeing her, you would have said there was just not enough girl there to pit against the thrust and slap of angry waves and relentless pressure of the winds prevailing across this tricky, punishing stretch of water. Perhaps her lack of beauty had something to do with her choice of ordeals. Certainly her decision to try to become the first woman to swim the English Channel was one of the most unselfish ones in the annals of sport. She wanted to accomplish this solely to bring a modicum of fame to the club she felt had done so much for her. She had not so much as the faintest foreshadowing of the celebrity it would make her personally, or the chance at fortune. And by that decision she touched off one of the supreme fairy tales of our times.

Trudy's specialty had always been long distance swimming; at the age of fourteen she had already made headlines by beating more than fifty opponents, including Britain's foremost girl swimmer, in a three-mile international race in New York Bay. A year or so later she swam from the Battery to Sandy Hook in record-breaking time. In 1925 the W.S.A. tapped its meager savings and Charlotte Epstein took Trudy Ederle abroad for her chance at the Channel.

No fanfare attended the attempt and even less its unhappy result. She failed. A turn in the tide accompanied by a sudden squall raised mountainous waves. Little more than half-conscious from nausea, waterlogged from the seas she had swallowed but still fighting, her limbs moving with indomitable automatism, she was pulled weeping and struggling from the Channel.

The naming of women as the weaker sex is a cliché which becomes even more frayed around the edges when such an example as that of Gertrude Ederle appears. In the failure this slight girl showed enough courage for a regiment, and displayed a fiber one never would have suspected in such a shy and otherwise ordinary person. Yet, as far as the American press and the rest of the world was concerned there was no story in defeat, and Miss Ederle was just another one of the many who had not swum the Channel.

There were two people, however, who were not convinced by this fiasco. One was Gertrude Ederle herself, and the other Captain Patterson of the *News*.

What brought these widely separated characters together was the fact that Channel swimming was an expensive business. There was transportation abroad and return, a long training period on the spot to become familiar with temperatures, eddies, rip tides, in short the nature of the enemy, the engaging of coaches and the hiring of accompanying craft. The resources of the Women's Swimming Association were insufficient to stand the cost of a second attempt. It was suggested to Captain Patterson that the *News* and the Chicago *Tribune* snydicate step in to back another try in exchange for the exclusive story should she succeed. With the prescience that made him the oustanding publisher he was, Captain Patterson agreed, gambling that if she made it, it would be the event of the year. But I doubt whether even he was aware of how big a story it would turn out to be.

A contract was prepared backing her with expenses, plus salary and a bonus. It called for a big decision on the part of an eighteen-year-old girl, for it meant giving up her amateur standing. Thereafter she would be a professional and denied all further amateur competition. It meant winner take all; loser forfeit everything. The iron determination and stubborn ambition concealed beneath that disarmingly gentle exterior left her no choice. She had challenged the Channel and she was unwaveringly resolved to defeat it. She signed.

We packed her off to Cap Gris Nez in France to train for her final effort. With her went her older sister, Margaret, herself a talented W.S.A. swimmer, Westbrook Pegler, then Chicago *Tribune* columnist and his wife, the late Julie Harpman, crack cityside reporter of the *News*. The coach who joined the party abroad was none other than that Thomas Burgess who, fifteen years before, had been the second to make the Channel crossing; his time, twenty-two hours and thirty-five minutes.

But in 1926 we were still innocents, not disillusioned. We had not yet had our noses rubbed into the fact that the dead of the 1914–18 war had indeed died in vain; that nothing whatsoever had been settled and that the democracies of the world were less safe than ever they had been before. To us virtue had scored a victory over evil in this war; white had beaten black, and we were established more firmly than ever in our belief in the favorite American fairy tale, the triumph of the artless good over the scheming iniquitous.

Such a story almost immediately began to build up at Cap Gris Nez, where the *News*-Chicago *Tribune*-Ederle party set up training quarters and Julie Harpman, covering, began to send home reports of cabals, disloyalties, and downright sabotage. We learned that our tender, guileless Trudy, the first All-American girl to arouse the nation to a frenzy of hysteria, had become enmeshed in a web of intrigue and hostility. In addition to having to contend with the furies of the Channel, it seemed there were those most necessary adjuncts of the bona fide *conte des fées,* ogres galore, and to the palpitating Americano, the best of all villains—furriners.

Neither the French nor the British wanted the girl to succeed in her attempt. As the *News* published Miss Harpman's stories with their unveiled hints of what was going on, the rest of the town and the country as well began to sit up and take notice, aware that being enacted daily before their eyes, as it were, and approaching its climax were all the elements of our most cherished type of dream. That climax failed no one.

The swim began the morning of August 6; the sea fairly calm, the forecast favorable. But weather prediction then was not what it is today. Evening and change of tide brought on a line squall, whipping the Channel into a hell of tide race and battering waves. With the chalk cliffs a few miles off Trudy would gain one yard and then lose two to the elements. Already the captain of the French escort tugboat had tried to break up the swim by bearing across her course until he was forcibly restrained by members of Trudy's party.

At twilight when she had been in the water for twelve hours, fighting fatigue, nausea, and all the devils of the deep against her, Thomas Burgess shouted from the tug that was lurching and wallowing in the heavy seas, "She must come out! But I will not take the responsibility of waiting for a sign from her indicating that she wishes to come out."

Whatever Burgess' motive might have been—perhaps sheer humanity rather than obstruction—it was the voice of authority and experience and once more the success of the adventure hung in the balance.

Someone leaned over the side and yelled into the teeth of the wind, "Trudy, you must come out!"

The girl raised her head out of the water and looked up from the deep trough of black waves, against which her legs were still threshing their six-beat trudgeon as regularly as the thumping of the engines from the accompanying vessel, and asked, "What for?"

With those two words, innocence and pluck triumphed. She battled onward. Two hours or so later Trudy walked out of the sea, up onto the sands of Dover to be met, I am afraid, if my memory is not tricking me, by a British immigration officer who solemnly kept her standing at the water's edge, demanding her passport, an idiocy which I note was repeated only this last summer in the case of another young girl swimmer who had just crossed for the exercise.

During her remarkable effort the story drove all other news off the front pages, and her feat was recorded in millions of words in thousands of columns of newspaper space. There had never been anything like it before.

In order to be the first to present the pictorial record of her accomplishment the *News*, as a picture paper, organized the swiftest and most expensive relay in the history of journalism up to that time. Sets of photographs were placed aboard four express liners departing from Southampton the same day. All of these were scheduled to arrive in New York simultaneously and practically at the same hour, which meant that our competition would have them as soon as we.

One of these ships, however, was a Canadian Pacific liner, an Empress steamer, whose destination was Montreal and thus, traveling the great circle route, reached the rim of the North American continent a day before the others. Employing two aircraft, one a sea and the other a land plane, a racing car with a famous driver, a railroad locomotive and an ambulance for the last leg, the photographs in waterproof wrapping were snatched from the ocean by the seaplane, where they were thrown overboard at the mouth of the St. Lawrence River, and then speeded on their relay through fog and dirty weather, to land in the *News* office twelve hours in advance of any others, a clean scoop. When we appeared on the street at eight o'clock that night with the picture of Gertrude Ederle greased, goggled, emerging from the sea near Dover, there was not another such picture in the

whole of the United States. However, just as a wry epilogue to
the journalism of those times, our competition, the rival *Mirror*,
simply photographed our front and back pages and reproduced
these in their next edition.

And thereafter all of America lay at her feet. The cornucopia
of plenty, beyond the most fantastic dreams, awaited her, ready
to be tipped and pour forth gold in an unending shower. She
was at that moment the most famous girl in the world and promoters were queuing up, checkbook in hand.

To handle her affairs and sift these offers the family had engaged the services of a smooth and coony lawyer, the late Dudley
Field Malone. But alas for Trudy, Mr. Malone was wise and
smoothly practiced mainly in the matter of securing Paris di-
vorces for American dollar princesses anxious to shed dull hus-
bands. As an international lawyer this was his specialty; he was
tops. But he was far from experienced in the handling of a new
kind of celebrity, and particularly one of the caliber of Gertrude
Ederle. So dazzled was he by the offers that came pouring in,
that instead of confirming the best and bona fide ones accompanied by cash deposits immediately and thus assuring his client
a lifetime competency, he held out for more. If so much was
being offered while Trudy was still wiping the protective layer
of grease from her body and shaking herself dry, how much more
would one not be able to glean when she returned to the
reception that was building up for her?

One can fault Mr. Malone for greed and inexperience, but it
must be remembered that the greed was on behalf of his client.
How was he to guess that the very sweetness, innocence, and
guilelessness that characterized Gertrude Ederle was to prove
his and her undoing and hand us our first jolt as to the in-
evitability of the happy ending?

For in spite of the furor that attended her achievement and
the urging of our own reportorial staff that she return immediately to the United States, Trudy remained unconvinced either
of her celebrity or the importance of cashing in at once. She
was a stubborn girl, too, in her simplicity, and instead of catching the first packet Sandy Hook-bound, she went off to some
little village in the Black Forest of Germany to pay a visit to

Grossmutterchen, her dear old grandmother, whom she had never seen. There she spent some three idyllic and fatal weeks, during which time a second woman swam the English Channel.

Her name was Mrs. Mille Gade Corson, and she was the mother of two children, the first mother, then, to swim the Channel. In those days the word "mother" was still sacred in the U.S., still a tear-jerker *par excellence.* Only a scant ten years before, vaudevillians had been warbling a lyric that went something like: "M-o-t-h-e-r spells mother, the sweetest word in the world to me," leaving not a dry eye in the house.

It took Mother Corson an hour longer to negotiate the twenty-one miles between Gris Nez and the white cliffs of Dover, but it rubbed the edge off Trudy's feat and knocked the bottom out of her market. She was no longer the only woman to have swum the Channel and thereby a salable freak for public exhibition. One by one the would-be entrepreneurs, who had been sitting hat in hand in Mr. Malone's antechamber, slipped away. The gold and silver that would have made her comfortable and independent for the rest of her life, turned to ashes.

Her welcome, when she finally did return, was unstinted, for American hearts then were not fickle, nor were they commercially involved. Her journey through the canyons of downtown Broadway brought forth a most tremendous outpouring of love from the people of New York, and the thunder of her name as they cheered the girl with the exalted, tear-stained face, rolled and echoed from side to side of the tall buildings.

And here the fairy tale should have ended with, "And she grew rich, married a prince, and lived happily ever after." But that wasn't how it went.

Once, she had named as her heart's desire a red Buick Roadster. As a bonus for her courage, determination, and success, Captain Patterson bought her one and it was waiting at the Battery for her when she disembarked from the *Macom.* Her "managers," who were engaged in keeping everyone away from her, would not even allow it to be presented by us, and she only received it late that night before the delicatessen shop on upper Amsterdam Avenue. And in effect it was all she ever got for her pains, beyond some chickenfeed for one or two endorsements and per-

And the reward. Trudy comes home.

sonal appearances, much of which she used to reimburse the Women's Swimming Association for their original outlay on her behalf.

The cruel buffeting she had taken on the sides of her head during that grueling crawl permanently affected her hearing. Later, during an aquatic performance, she hurt her back and spent eight months in a plaster cast. A professional henceforth and forced to earn a living, she took a job as a swimming instructress to teach the young and quietly disappeared into the limbo of the forgotten—forgotten, that is, by all but her own friends.

She never complained about those who had mishandled and failed her. She remained wholly unspoiled by the great outpouring of adulation and publicity. She was never bitter, rude, or snobbish, nor wavered in that buoyancy and essential innocence which marked her character. The golden decade reached its end and America entered the crucible of change. Gertrude Ederle, for one, emerged from it a greater human being and one of the true Golden ones of the era.

Jack the Giant Killer.

Young man from Manassa.

CHAPTER 4

Jack Dempsey

During my thirteen-year tenure at the sports desk of the *Daily News*, I saw Jack Dempsey fight only four times. In those four bouts he was defeated twice and in the other two, which he won by knockouts, each time he came close to being knocked out himself.

Yet, of all the fighters I have ever known and heavyweight champions I have seen in action, Dempsey still rules over my imagination as the greatest, most exciting and dramatic.

And here again you must not think I am trying to say that fighters then were better or harder hitters than ours of today, and perhaps Sonny Liston would have made mincemeat of Dempsey (or perhaps not?). My story is that in addition to being the heavyweight champion of the world, Jack Dempsey was a tremendous personality, one of the most engaging and arresting in the entire realm of what we considered the giants of sports of the 1920s.

And, for that matter, he still is. The old magic still clings to him as it did in the years back, even long after his retirement. I had the most astonishing example of this when I visited him in April 1964 at his restaurant on Broadway in the fifties. The place was packed at the luncheon hour with visitors from out of town. The great majority of them were middle-aged women who must have been little girls, or infants in arms back in the twenties, Dempsey's heyday.

One would have thought that his customers would have been drawn largely from the old-timers among the men who remembered him as the hero of their youth, and would visit him to

The glowering visage of Lucifer, the Dark Angel.

Background for the sleep producer.

shake his hand and hear him say, "Well, hello there! How's my old pal from Ashtabula?"

But no, the place was filled instead with clucking hens who were there, I suspect, not because of what Dempsey once was, but for what he still is today, a virile, male animal with a powerful attraction for the female sex.

He was always a spectacular person with an extraordinarily dynamic aura, and I was aware of this from the very first when I knew him as a young man.

When he entered a crowded room or enclosure, such as a gathering after a football game, or a World Series, suddenly there was no one else but Jack Dempsey there. All others, celebrity, star, champion, or ex-champion faded into insignificance before the amazing magnetism of this dark-haired, dark-visaged man with the lithe, panther-like movements and the quick, friendly smile. He was never less than twelve feet tall.

He overshadowed his era, which stretched roughly from July 4, 1919, when he knocked out Jess Willard, until 1932, when he retired for the last time. He served as creator, actor, villain, and hero in a thrilling human story whose excitement and import extended far beyond prize fighting. At the end he became inextricably enmeshed with another engrossing, true-to-life melodrama, that of his successor and the man who dethroned him, Gene Tunney.

It may be difficult for this generation to understand how involved all of us were at one time or another, in some way, with the Dempsey story and how many people, men, women, and children, who never even came near to a prize ring or an arena, or ever saw a gloved blow struck, were influenced by him and felt the impact of his individuality, his rise and his fall.

Our whole approach at that time to boxing, prize fighting, and the striking of a man with the closed fist is involved here and will bear a moment's digression, for in this second half of the twentieth century I suspect we do not entertain the same feelings with regard to the value of the punch on the nose as a settler of arguments, or a genuinely disabling element. But there was a time when, in our national thinking, imagination, and behavior, the human fist loomed as the *ne plus ultra* of

weapons. The accepted method of replying to an insult, or dealing with a cad, was to knock the fellow down.

Fist fighting as a game is an ancient affair. The Etruscans,
who antedated the Romans, practiced it, their hands protected
with soft bandages. The Romans elevated the sport by reinforc-
ing these bandages with iron, and the cestus was developed
which did away with arguments on who won the fight by caving
in the side of a man's head with one successful blow.

The Romans have always been reviled for the brutality of this
development of the so-called art of boxing, but actually they
might be considered quite sensible. They merely carried the
implication of the game, the purpose of which was to disable a
man, a step farther, cutting out a great deal of the intermediate
torture suffered by practitioners, say even today, in a fifteen-
round bout with six-ounce gloves. Wearing the cestus, the
question as to which was the better man was settled quickly
and once and for all.

Barbarians they might have been, those who overran the
Roman Empire and brought about its downfall, but they were
not so stupid as to adopt this peculiar form of entertainment,
and it certainly had no value for them in warfare. And this is
the last we hear of men fighting one another with their fists
until some fifteen hundred or so years later when we come to
the bare-knuckle days of the English prize ring, where men
once more resumed the folly of beating one another about the
head and body with their clenched hands.

It was an era which saw the lethal sword finally retired to
the fencing *salle,* and man's eternal aggressiveness expressed
traditionally with the punch.

Aboard the clipper ships it was, "Blow the man down" when
insubordination threatened, though it was as often accomplished
with a belaying pin or marlin spike as by the first mate's
knuckles. In the roaring logging and mining camps of the American West, no man was a man who was not handy with his
dukes, though once a fellow had been floored it was not considered inelegant to stamp upon his features with a hobnailed
boot. Gouging and biting were usual in a barroom brawl.

But what emerged as part and parcel of the century's turn

was fisticuffs: John L. Sullivan, rattling the chandeliers of saloons with his bellow of, "I can lick any man in the house!" the invitation to "Step outside," and the street corner fight in which a couple of argumentative truck drivers would "square off" against one another, their hands raised in attitudes reminiscent of old prints depicting Sayres vs. Heenan. Down South, gentlemen still refused to soil their hands, and when their feelings were hurt, resorted to the pistol or the horsewhip to erase the stain. But in the North it was the punch aimed at the point of the jaw which decided issues.

By the 1920s, barroom brawling and the personal fist fight were no longer in style, but the memories lingered on, and when prize fighting became legalized with stuffed gloves drawn over bare knuckles, three-minute rounds, and rules and regulations by a British peer, the Marquis of Queensberry, thousands were enabled to enjoy vicariously what was no longer considered *de rigueur* socially. From the security of a ringside seat we could participate in and savor all of the thrill of a well-timed, well-aimed blow landing flush on the button, to knock a man into oblivion. We were back again with our friends, the early Etruscans.

To still the outcries of the soft-hearted and pious and the general meddlers, boxing was presented as "the manly art of self-defense" and cited as health-giving and character-building. Nothing, of course, could have been more ridiculous or farther from the truth. Boxing at all times, except when the Romans pepped it up with their little variation of cast-iron gloves, has been a most inadequate means of combat. It has no more to do with self-defense than a soldier attacking a tank with a peashooter. When one considers modern guerrilla training and the many ways of disabling a man, often permanently, that have been developed, the punch seems little less than puerile.

I have never heard the absurdities of boxing better capsuled than by a little fellow, a Frenchman named Monsieur Léon See. M. See was the first discoverer and manager of Primo Carnera, a gargantuan travesty of a prize fighter who flourished in the post-Dempsey era; a snaggle-toothed, oversized, behemoth of a man who stood six feet five, weighed 270 pounds, and actually couldn't fight a lick. The axiom of M. See, which I have never forgotten, was, "The head was not meant to be punched and the fist was never intended by nature to be a weapon."

He was, of course, 100 per cent right on both counts. Blows about the head invariably cause a series of traumas and lesions in the brain which result in the miserable, shuffling, semi-idiotic condition of punch-drunkenness. And what more preposterous striking weapon could you envisage than one composed of dozens of small, fragile bones and cartilages which comprise fingers, knuckles, and the back of the hand, attached to a mechanism even more delicate, the human wrist?

Fifty years has seen a considerable change in the concept of self-defense, and the reply to any kind of a personal attack to-day would be to discourage the attacker with something solid, such as a chair, a bottle or any handy piece of metal. Or, if this were not available, to kick him in the conclusive spot, a guarantee of bringing the argument to a close.

The particular sensitivity of man's most prized possessions was recognized by the regulators of prize ring boxing and were ruled out of bounds.

It was a regulation, incidentally, to which most fighters never entirely subscribed, and one method of studying their opponent's character in the ring was to touch him up once or twice in that region to see whether he could take it. In spite of the rule giving them protection against this type of assault—if you were actually disabled by a blow in that quarter, you were awarded the fight on a foul—fighters wore metal cups inside their trunks for protection. Further, to make life somewhat less hazardous to the boxer, kidney punches and rabbit punches (blows struck to the cervical column at the back of the neck) were barred, but never once during my thirteen-year stint in the sports chair at the *News,* in which time I must have witnessed literally thousands of prize fights, did I ever see a professional contestant warned for bashing his opponent one in the kidneys or batting him on the neck during a clinch. Body punching was quite permissible, and if a kidney happened to get in the way it was bad luck. In fact, an accepted technique of this healthful and character-building sport was to slug a man's stomach, liver,

Savage tiger. Dempsey before the Firpo fight.

pancreatic, and kidney areas until he became so weak that he either collapsed from this treatment, spread over a period of up to fifteen three-minute rounds, or dropped his hands and opened up his chin for the brain-destroying quietus.

So much for some of the physiology of this so-called sport. But to all of us who were young, or even middle-aged, at the beginning of the Golden Decade, the boxing champion was the symbol of manliness, courage, and virility. He was greatly admired and as the sport became respectable, this admiration resulted in hitherto unheard-of sums of money for the prize fighter.

How the game was made respectable will be told in the reminiscence of Tex Rickard, a promoter. But how it brought drama into everyday, humdrum existence as well as the vicarious sharing of the life and emotions and the physical prowess of the most elemental and destructive ringman of his time, belongs to the enthralling serial story of Jack Dempsey. This took place before our eyes and in our midst mainly over those exciting ten years.

In the days of Jem Mace, Tom Cribb, Sayres, Heenan, Molineaux, and similar bare-knuckle fighters who performed for Beau Brummel and other Regency dandies and British sports, the occupation with the prize ring was largely an excuse for the exchange of wagers and a kind of clinical interest in how long men could last in fights that went on for as many as seventy, eighty, or a hundred rounds. A round terminated when one or the other, or both, of the battlers hit the turf, either knocked or thrown down. Certain professional bullies enjoyed aristocratic patronage but concern for them, their characters, or their lives there was none, and in this they resembled the paid gladiators of ancient times. It was the immediate outcome of the match that mattered and not the participants, or how they might be affected.

It was not until 1892, when Gentleman Jim Corbett, a speedy, dapper, trimly muscled Fancy Dan, knocked out the beefy, beery, hitherto unbeatable heavyweight champion of the world, John L. Sullivan, that it was first suspected that there might be a dramatic tale in the personality and background of the fighter himself. Thereafter the combination of legalized boxing following upon World War I, the removal of much of the social ostracism connected with its earlier and more sordid days, and the appearance upon the scene of men who not only had stories but who also *were* stories, and lived them right out in the glaring spotlight of increased newspaper publicity, inaugurated the most flourishing and thrilling era in the entire history of fist fighting.

At one championship prize fight, when the challenger was knocked to the floor, I heard and saw a sportswriter arise in his Working Press seat and scream at the dazed and stricken man writhing on the canvas, "Stay down, you tin-canning son-of-a-bitch!"

Here was a moment of pure and personal identification. For the fallen man had never worked any harm upon the sportswriter. They were not personal enemies. But the writer loved and admired the champion and was anathematizing and putting the gypsy curse on his opponent, so that the man he idolized might win. And in some respect the writer was even the champion himself, a hairsbreadth away from victory and no doubt saying to himself, as so many fighters have and do when they have managed to tip their adversaries over with a blow—"Stay down, you son-of-a-bitch!"

If a hardened sportswriter could find himself prey to such violent emotions and uncontrolled outbursts, what about the public, fed day in and day out upon newspaper stories pertaining to their favorites, written by the same inspired and adulating reporters?

The feeling of knowing the heavyweight champion of the world intimately, his virtues, his failings, his strength and his weakness, over a long period of time helped to draw the greatest crowds in the history of the prize ring to see him perform. There was more newspaper space to devote to these characters in those times, and more reason for allotting it, since the interest in such a man as Dempsey was constant and usually at fever heat. The result of this was that when he went into battle there was more than a title at stake. The human being whom we either loved or detested, admired or despised, was entering a kind of public ordeal and we simply had to be there, either in person or by the proxy of our newspapers or radio.

And whether or not one approved of prize fights, Jack Dempsey in association with his clever, cunning manager and alter ego, Jack Kearns, created the dramatic image of the perfect pugilist and more than this, he was Jack the Giant Killer who tumbled into the dust men who outsized and outweighed him.

My old friend will kill me for this, but he was a man of extraordinary beauty as well as virility, and if this is not the word, you, who remember him as he was in his prime, find me a better one. It was beauty in the sense of perfect proportion and the rugged, glowering visage of Lucifer, the Dark Angel; his hair blue-black, his eyes dark and snapping, the mouth cruel and determined, the chin stubborn. In his face was the best of two handsome races, the Celt and the American aborigine. His father was a West Virginia mountain man with some Choctaw blood. From his mother he inherited a Cherokee strain.

Dempsey's body was magnificently put together, trim, tapered at the waist, smoothly muscled, nothing of the bruiser or strong man about the frame or biceps, very little indeed to indicate the destroyer he was. In fact, when matched against some of the giants of the game he looked like a lightweight.

Into the ring with him he carried a swelling truculence that surged up from deep inside him somewhere, exploding into unimaginable violence which found an echo in the aggressiveness lurking in every male. It was this link between the attacker on the platform and the spectators that brought the crowd roaring to its feet, experiencing vicariously this unquenchable ferocity as a personal catharsis.

Dempsey, like many champions, was not always popular because of two main issues, neither of which was valid. One was his record in World War I and the other his alleged avoidance of a Negro heavyweight challenger by the name of Harry Wills.

Regarding the affair of World War I, there was a dark shadow behind Dempsey, like Mephisto at the elbow of Dr. Faustus. His name was Jack Kearns, manager. Kearns had not nursed and raised a million-dollar heavyweight championship prospect to be a target for something a boxer couldn't block—shot and shell. And so he put him into a shipyard and gave him a riveter's gun, instead of a khaki uniform and a rifle.

This was indeed naughty and reprehensible but the blame

Tame tiger. Dempsey with Estelle Taylor just before their marriage. Left to right: Mrs. Frances Carter (Estelle Taylor's sister), Estelle, Dempsey and Dempsey's sister Elsie.

must rest upon Kearns and not on Dempsey. The former was never exactly a sweet-smelling article except when, as was his habit, he dowsed himself with *eau de cologne.* He was devious, untruthful, unscrupulous, but quick-witted, and everything else that a great manager of a prize fighter ought to be.

In his early days Dempsey was completely untutored and ignorant, not only in the ways of the prize ring, but of the world as well. Kearns who, from the very beginning of their association, was getting him more money for bouts than he ever dreamed existed, seemed a super brain to him and he was content to put himself wholly into his hands. Whenever Dempsey was asked about anything he would say invariably, "Talk to Kearns. He's the doctor," from which Kearns eventually derived his nickname, "Doc."

If the Doc made an egregious error with the shipyard business, it must be remembered that right up to our actual involvement in World War I we were singing a popular song entitled, "I Didn't Raise My Boy To Be A Soldier," which largely expressed the national sentiment until replaced by the trumpet call of George M. Cohan's "Over There!" We were pacifist, constantly quoting George Washington's strictures against becoming involved in foreign wars, and a large part of the population was pro-German as well.

Neither Kearns and certainly not the naïve Dempsey were bright enough to guess that within a year those same moms who had not raised their boys to be soldiers would turn into female, recruiting harpies, harrying young men into uniform and chanting lays about what we were going to do to Kaiser Bill. The truth was that there was not an ounce of beagle in Dempsey ever. He was no more afraid of being a soldier than he was of being a fighter, as he proved when, in World War II, as a Commander in the U. S. Coast Guard on an inspection tour in the Pacific, he jumped ship to mingle in the desperate struggle for Okinawa.

It was unforgivably stupid of the otherwise clever Kearns so to damage the image of his meal-ticket. For had he permitted Dempsey to enlist, his charge would probably have faced no dangers greater than that of becoming an athletic or boxing instructor in some soldier camp. And yet even this piece of idiocy

could be turned into gold in those postwar days. For when Tex
Rickard matched Dempsey with the Frenchman Georges Carpentier at Boyle's 30 Acres in Jersey City in 1921, the result was
the first million-dollar gate in the history of prize fighting. As a
matter of fact, so many wanted to see Dempsey the villain get
his from hero Carpentier, that the gate was only two hundred
thousand short of *two* million dollars.

Ringwise it was a gross mismatch, Carpentier being little more
than a heavy middleweight. But in those days the scenario was
the magnet that drew record crowds to the box office. Once the
bell rang, Dempsey threw away the script and dealt romance a
body blow by knocking the Frenchman kicking in four rounds,
after having received and weathered only one serious right-hand
punch from his lighter opponent.

What price, then, Kearns' error? Dempsey's share of this gate
was close to a third of a million dollars.

It was equally ridiculous to charge that Dempsey was afraid
to defend his title against Harry Wills. Black and white was a
political football then, as it is now, though for different reasons.
We, who have lived comfortably and pleasurably under the long
reign of Joe Louis and now are subjects of heavyweights Sonny
Liston and Cassius Clay (whichever one happens to have pos-
session of the ball at the moment) cannot imagine how nervous
and squeamish we were then at the thought of another Negro
heavyweight champion. This was due perhaps in part to the unfortunate behavior of white and black during the tenure of Jack
Johnson from 1908 to 1915. I remember in my boyhood days a
period of national idiocy when every up-and-coming Caucasian
heavyweight was dubbed a White Hope.

Again the facts are that Dempsey was no more afraid of
fighting Harry Wills than he was of fighting anyone else. Actually
Tex Rickard never wanted to promote a Dempsey-Wills fight
and when pressure of public opinion, whipped up by newspaper
criticism, forced Kearns to sign Dempsey for a Wills bout, William Muldoon, then chairman of the New York State Athletic
Commission, forbade the fight. No one behaved normally or
sensibly during this curious period, but it was Dempsey who was
wrongly pilloried.

From the battle of the Long Count, seventh round: Tunney (white trunks) on his way down from a series of left and right hooks.

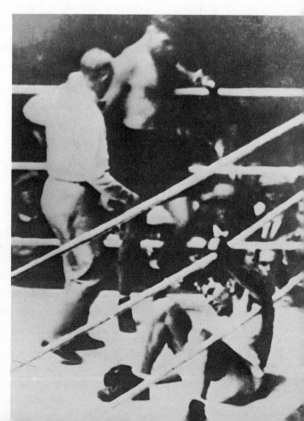

The man who didn't go to a neutral corner. Tunney gains valuable seconds while the referee persuades Dempsey to cross to the other side of the ring.

The count begins at last, but Tunney already has had five or six precious seconds to recover.

The result of the Long Count and Dempsey's failure to retire immediately to the neutral corner. Tunney floors Jack with a right-hand punch for no count and saves his title.

I saw and met Dempsey for the first time during the summer of 1923 when, as a raw cub reporter from the sports department, I was sent to Saratoga Springs to write some color stories on his training camp. I braced him one hot afternoon on the porch of his cottage to ask him whether he would spar a round with me to enable me to write a story about it. I remember how he looked, not quite as tall as I, clad in an old, gray sweater, still crinkle-nosed then, three days' growth of beard, with his curiously high-pitched voice and body always restless and moving.

Much has been written about Dempsey in his heyday, about his viciousness, his cruelty, and the killer in him, but the truth is that he was basically a good-hearted man. It was a kindly act for him to consent, on the eve of an important defense of his title, to take on an unknown reporter in order that he might not fail in his assignment; one, incidentally, who stood an inch and a half taller and outweighed him by ten pounds.

You might not consider it a kindness to deal out a split lip, a bloody nose, and a knockout, left hook to the chin to a tyro, but it is results that count, and the ten seconds I spent unconscious on the canvas were the turning point of my career. For so amused was Captain Patterson by the affair that shortly afterward he made me sports editor and gave me a daily column to write. It was also one of the few instances when Dempsey stood out against his manager, for Kearns, who was absent at my first meeting with Jack, when the champion agreed to take me on, was furious when he heard of the proposed bout. He pointed out the risk that Dempsey was taking of a possible injury at the hands of one who might be a ringer. I was at the time unknown, weighed a fit 195 pounds, having just graduated from the captaincy of the Columbia crew, and even looked something like a fighter, a resemblance which ended abruptly when the first Dempsey hook bounced off my chin. Dempsey's reply was to the effect that he had agreed to take me on and that he did not go back on his word.

The first fight in which I ever saw Dempsey engage was that tremendous, heart-stopping brawl at the Polo Grounds in New York City on the night of September 14, 1923, against Luis Angel Firpo, which was rightly called the Battle of the Century, for nothing like it has been seen since for thrills, chills, and pure animal savagery, unleashed over a period of three minutes and fifty-eight seconds. In this uninhibited contest there was revealed a barbarity that echoed the earliest battles of primitive man or the awful, slashing, death struggle of wild beasts hidden in the depths of some jungle. Indeed, the giant Firpo had been nick-named and likened to a wild bull and if this was so, Dempsey was the tiger attacking for the kill.

In that opening round, which surpassed even the one at Toledo in which Dempsey wrecked the huge Willard, Firpo was knocked down six times and Dempsey twice; the latter once at the be-ginning for no count, by the first punch thrown by Firpo, and the second time near the close, when he was swept completely from the ring by the Argentine's blind rush and clubbing right. Pushed back onto the platform by sportswriters (more in self-defense than in an attempt to aid him), he made it to his feet before "ten" and then, though stunned and no more than semi-conscious, was carrying the fight to the giant when the bell ended the most thrilling first round in the history of the prize ring. In his corner Dempsey was still half out; he didn't know what round it was, what day of the week, or what town he was in either. Yet he rose at the bell with renewed fury to drop Firpo twice more, the last time for the full count.

This was Dempsey's great appeal to us all, the sustained pug-nacity that swept him from his corner, heedless of defense, to slug, punch, and batter until his opponent no longer remained before him. In the heat of battle the niceties of ring comportment went by the board. Often many of the blows he sprayed from his weaving, cat-like crouch were low. Against Firpo, half-mad-dened by battle lust, he stood over the fallen challenger when he knocked him down, instead of retiring to a corner for the count, and slugged him again when he had barely regained his feet. And once even stood behind him and hit him on the rise. The referee, himself stunned by the fury of the fight in which he found himself involved, let Dempsey get away with it.

No one at that time could guess that these actions would one day cost Dempsey the regaining of his lost world's championship, when failure to heed the rule to go to a neutral corner resulted in the famous Chicago long count when he had Gene Tunney on the floor, knocked out, in their second fight, only to have him recover and come on to win.

But no one ever heard William Harrison Dempsey ask for quarter either, or complain of a low punch. After the Chicago affair he admitted that what happened had been his own fault and that was the end of it.

During that great, rambunctious decade Dempsey appeared in one million-dollar extravaganza after another; the heavy in one, hero and leading man in the next. We have seen how he was cast as the villain against Georges Carpentier. He was hero again, and Jack-the-Giant-Killer, against Firpo, who outweighed him by twenty-two pounds and towered over him as well. Yet, when he entered the ring for his title defense against Gene Tunney at Philadelphia, it was Tunney, the underdog, the ex-Marine of World War I, who was cast in the role of leading man. The publicists had revived not only the war-time charges against Dempsey, but the equally untrue bill that he had avoided Harry Wills, his most persistent Negro challenger.

At the end of the ten rounds in which Tunney staggered the experts and the spectators by outboxing Dempsey, battering one side of his face to a pulp and taking his title away from him, it needed only a single gesture to turn the tables of popularity. Back in the hotel that night his wife, the glamorous motion picture star Estelle Taylor, asked, "What happened, Ginsberg?" (her pet name for him). Dempsey grinned a crooked smile with the good side of his face and said, "Honey, I forgot to duck." The nation took the beaten villain to its heart, loved him again, and dubbed him hero. We were that naïve and that fickle.

Hero, Dempsey remained then, through the night he fought ex-sailor Jack Sharkey to earn his return bout with champion Gene Tunney. It was another million-dollar gate, a crowd of 75,000, and of this maybe there were probably no more than five thousand souls who wanted to see Sharkey win.

In this bout Dempsey came within an ace of being destroyed in the first round, in which Sharkey dealt out such punishment that Jack was barely able to wobble to his corner at its end. But it was another one of those battles so characteristic of the times, when it was the story that mattered; the ex-champion making his comeback.

It seemed that Dempsey could hardly survive another round, yet he did and subsequent ones as well, managing to regain sufficient strength to indulge in several of his exploratory probes to test out just how much character boxing had built into his opponent. In the seventh round he found out. Sharkey applied to the referee for help, foolishly dropping his hands and turning his head to the arbiter to complain of the low punches, thus offering Dempsey a gratis shot at his wide-open chin. Gratefully accepting the invitation, Dempsey left-hooked him into the ten-second oblivion and won the fight. Nobody gave a damn that night whether Dempsey's punches were high or low. Dempsey was our boy. He won!

And hero he remained up to and through the famous Battle of the Long Count in Chicago, where for all of Tunney's boxing skill, he set the crowd of 105,000 partisans aflame with excitement when, in the seventh round, like the Dempsey of old, he slugged Tunney to the floor and then threw away certain victory with his old habit of standing over his opponent. The precious seconds ticked away while Referee Dave Barry kept motioning him to a neutral corner until he obeyed, enabling Tunney's superb recuperative powers to take effect. And thereafter during the rest of that round and Tunney's equally famous back-pedaling flight to victory, the final affecting image was created of the old mauler whose aging, tired legs had failed him, stopping in mid-ring, a look of contempt on his face, motioning with his gloved hands for Tunney to stop running and come in and fight.

Dempsey retired after this battle of September 1927 but was persuaded to begin a comeback tour which started during the summer of 1931 and which ended exactly a year later. During this tour he met some 175 opponents, sometimes taking on three and four a night, and knocked out over a hundred of them. This was perhaps his most remarkable achievement. None of these were heavyweights of note, or had been heard of before, but alone for a thirty-six-year-old fighter to bounce that much beef onto the canvas in a year must be accredited as sensational. In 1932 he took on a fair-to-middling heavyweight, Kingfish Levinsky, and when

"The lives of the two were inextricably woven together."

he was outpointed by him, listened to the message of lost speed
and hung up his gloves for good—a man rich, respected, and
loved to this day.

For after all, his was one of the first of the great American
sports success stories. He had fulfilled every requirement of the
legend, having come up the hard way, a poor boy from the rough
mining camps and clapboard ranching towns of the Far West to
become a giant killer and a millionaire.

But he did more than just fulfill our romantic notions; he provided a reflection of what we hoped was our own masculinity
and imagined prowess when it came to "upping" to another male
and letting him have it. In the safe haven of the mind we were
Dempseys all, dark destroyers against whose flying fists no man
could stand. Jack, who believed that the best defense was attack,
along with his willingness to take three to give one, dealt a considerable blow to the theory of the Manly Art of Self-Defense,
whose greatest exponent was his twice-conqueror, Gene Tunney.
But it was in the end the image of Dempsey which nurtured
our aggressions and stoked our imaginations with the destructive
and explosive bursts of punches he fired against the giants of the
ring and which have never been forgotten.

Who, in our times, would not have wanted to be like Jack
Dempsey?

The All-American Boy.

CHAPTER **5**

Gene Tunney

It is, of course, impossible to tell the story of Jack Dempsey without combining it with that of James Joseph Tunney. For the lives of the two for a decade were inextricably woven together; they were so necessary to one another to enable them to meet their destinies, it seemed, almost as though some witch or wizard had attended the cradle of each and muttered a spell that united them at the peak of their careers, or that they had been invented for one another.

Each was at one time the heavyweight champion of the world, Tunney the successor to Dempsey. Both became millionaires out of their earnings in the prize ring. And they differed from each other as night does from day.

If, looking into the mirror held up by the beetling, lethal figure of Dempsey, we saw the image of what we hoped we might be like if ever we were called upon to fight with our fists, the glass presented by Gene Tunney revealed quite another reflection, one which we were at great pains vigorously and almost childishly to deny.

I remember so vividly how Tunney was pilloried, ridiculed, and abused on the sports pages, as well as his unpopularity with most of the fight fans of the times. Yet therefrom hangs one of the most extraordinary tales of the Glittering Twenties, a *True Confessions* type of romance which, had it been offered as fiction to an editor, would have been turned down as purest corn.

Synopsized, it would have read: Poor but proud pugilist falls in love with millionaire society girl; determines to become millionaire himself before suing for her hand; self-educates himself by

The fighting face of
James Joseph Tunney.

In action. The man on the floor is Georges Carpentier.

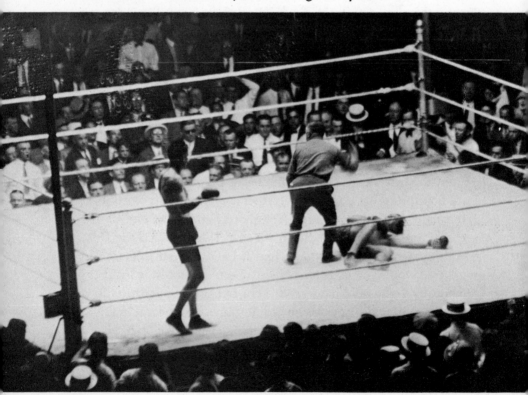

And in repose. Tunney the prize fighter who was hated because he liked to read.

reading good books while fighting his way to position as challenger to the heavyweight champion; meets brutal and savage knockout king in title match, outsmarts, outboxes him to take crown; defeats him again in return match; earns million dollars for thirty-minute fight; retires from ring; marries girl; lives happily ever after.

And this is exactly what happened.

The key to the persecution of Gene Tunney was that early in his life as a professional pugilist he was caught with a book in his hands. And, furthermore, to condemn him forever in the eyes of that generic fellow known as "the fight fan" was the fact that the book had been written by William Shakespeare. This crime haunted him through his entire career, and I am certain there was many a dolt who lost good money on the first Dempsey-Tunney fight because he would not bet on a fighter who had been found with his nose buried in *Coriolanus* or *Love's Labour's Lost*. When it came to a rough-and-tumble between a tough, ignorant back-woodsman and a fancy-pants with book-larnin', you put your money on the former every time.

It is difficult today to realize that less than fifty years ago we had not yet wholly emerged from that juvenile approach to learn-ing and literature which characterized the U.S.A. toward the end of the nineteenth century.

At that time a college man was largely looked down upon as a sissy in a turtle-necked sweater, or clad in blazer and boater. Even in the universities themselves, "grind" was a dirty word de-noting a bespectacled weakling, who spent his time swotting calculus and the shepherd kings of the Hyksos, instead of per-mitting his face to be ground into the mud of the football field like every other manly fellow.

In the early days of America education was a difficult thing to come by, and those who managed to acquire it were often looked upon with suspicion. Your man who could carve out tract, cabin, and corn field from the wilderness with his bare hands was the honest and trustworthy one, and according to the legend of the land, straightforward, simple, and undevious. The hang-over lasted for a long time, and it is only in recent years that the comic magazines dared to print jokes about the stupidity of big, beefy, thick-headed football players.

The gulf between town and gown, student and tough in those days was unbridgeable, and the sympathies and hidden feelings of the majority were with the he-man who represented our own pioneer conquest of the backlands.

Somehow, too, we thrived upon another fallacy, namely that sexual prowess was connected with bulging muscles and hairy

chests, sweat, and ignorance. One of the great literary successes
of the period was a novel by Ethel M. Dell entitled *The Sheik*,
in which a British lady succumbed upon a pile of carpets to the
ardor of a smelly but virile Arabian child of nature. Anything
which smacked of grace, intelligence, gentleness, and good manners seemed to have become linked with sexual debility. I remember how desperately frightened we all were in the days of my
own boyhood of being dubbed sissy, la-de-da, or effeminate. We
had to have a symbol of manliness to shore us up. Jack Dempsey
was that symbol.

Tunney was despised for his bookishness and the coupling of
his name with that of Shakespeare, at the same time that he was
enthralling us with his dramatic enactment of our very own favorite fairy tale, popularized by Burt L. Standish, Horatio Alger,
Jr. and other creators of healthy books for growing boys. Gene
certainly has us caught up in the ambivalence of the century. For
if ever there was a specimen, and example who typified Frank
Merriwell, the Rover Boys, and the All-American lad rolled into
one, it was James Joseph Tunney.

He was born in Lower New York of Irish-American parents in
1898 and by inclination and character seemed headed for the
priesthood. Even as a young boy he was an avid reader, browsing through the libraries of friends in the Village. Employed as
a clerk in a downtown shipping office, with the advent of World
War I he enlisted and went overseas with the U. S. Marines.
Boxing was a regular part of Marine training. Tunney won the
lightweight championship of the A.E.F. This success, apparently,
determined him to follow the game as his profession.

Tunney not only was, but looked the part of the new, True-
Blue American hero type as delineated in those days by artists
Charles Dana Gibson, James Montgomery Flagg, George Leyen-
decker, and others. He was tall, slender, extraordinarily handsome, square-jawed, crew-cut, with clear, fearless, gray eyes set
wide apart in a frank and open countenance. He had all the assets
of the romantic, priggish, impossible, juvenile fictional hero
which, for the half-century from the 1880s to the 1920s became
the model for American youth. Anyone checking his rise from
humble beginning to wealth and fame would find a man imbued

with loyalty, a sense of duty, self-confidence, initiative, burning ambition, indomitable courage, complete and utter fearlessness, and considerable self-satisfaction.

Added to this, by intelligence, study, and practice, he made himself into one of the best exponents of the so-called Manly Art of Self-Defense who ever laced on the red leather mittens. He was the absolute *ne plus ultra* of what a boxer ought to be.

Theoretically the perfect boxer would emerge from every test unscathed, even untouched by any blow, while leaving his opponent wrecked, bleeding, and unconscious on the canvas. Again, in theory, with speed of foot, hand, and eye it is possible to avoid every hook, cross, or uppercut by blocking with glove or arm, or slipping, ducking, pulling out of range—making the hitter miss. No one was ever *that* good at the game, but among the heavyweights Gene Tunney probably came closest to it. At the peak of his career he had learned to do everything that a master ringman should.

And "learned" was the operative word, for Tunney was never a natural fighter, born to the sport. On the contrary, he was synthetic, and he acquired the mechanics of his trade through long, bitter hours of practice, trial, and error. During his error periods he absorbed some pretty bad beatings, notably at the hands of an unorthodox middleweight by the name of Harry Greb. For hour upon hour he rehearsed every move of the game, the left lead, the right-hand follow-through, the hook, the uppercut, slipping, blocking with gloves, forearms, elbows, and shoulders; he ran backward for miles to obtain the stamina to retreat in the ring when necessary; he pickled his hands to harden them. He was a walking book entitled *How to Box.*

When we should have been cheering him to the echo for the perfection of his profession, we hated him instead for working his deceitful arts upon that hero image of ourselves, caveman Dempsey.

This image, incidentally, during that period was a fickle and sometime thing which could be equally represented by a Douglas Fairbanks, Sr., clevering his way on the silent screen through multitudes of swordsmen or hordes of villains. In football we often preferred the figure of Red Grange, the agile avoider of the armored brutes endeavoring to throw him down, over the line-crashing human tank. But when it came to fighting, it was the knocker-outer for us every time. You simply cannot imagine the satisfaction that swept through the majority of 105,000 souls packed into Soldier Field that night of September 22, 1927 when in that famous seventh round Dempsey broke through Tunney's exquisite defense with a series of stunning hooks and set the champion on his tail.

It is difficult now to remember, when trying to analyze the unpopularity of so noble-appearing a Roman as Gene, which came first, the chicken or the egg. Did some of the contempt for Tunney follow the lead of a number of sportswriters, among whom Westbrook Pegler of the Chicago *Tribune* and myself of the *Daily News* were the most scathing? Or was it we who, appraising the popular temper, tried to write what people seemed to be thinking and feeling?

And what about the storms and charges that swelled around Tunney's head during those days, that he had underworld connections, that he availed himself of gangster "protection," that he engaged set-ups to go into the tank for him to build up his reputation. There was simply no logic to the reactions which the strange, contradictory personality of Tunney aroused in us. On the one hand we bitterly resented Kid Galahad, while on the other we insisted he behave like same. We hated him for not acting boorishly, the way we felt a prize fighter should, and we despised him equally when in another area, he was accused of doing so. The poor man could not win, except in the ring when they rang the bell and turned him loose.

If there is anything easier to organize than a crooked horse race, it is a crooked prize fight. Every generation during which boxing has flourished has known them, including our present one. But in each era it had a different aspect and was managed in a different manner.

For instance, in the old days of the Horton and Frawley Laws when boxing was disreputable, attended by only a few sports and their molls and purses were picayune, the thievery was strictly petty and for peanuts. But later, throughout that extraordinary decade when the holding, or fighting for, a world's

The kind of people who admired and respected Tunney—Secretary of the Navy Wilbur and Major General John A. Lejeune, Commandant of the Marine Corps.

heavyweight championship involved millions of dollars for the first time, the larceny very quickly became grand. With previously unheard-of sums of money bestowed upon champions of every class, and even flyweights pecking at one another for stakes of several hundred thousand dollars, boxing became big business in the hands of men whose ethics had never been exactly sound or admirable.

For that matter, one suspects that in any kind of commerce, when a million dollars knocks at the door, ethics might conceivably take flight via the window. When no more than a hundred-dollar club fight was involved you could afford to send your boy in to take his chances on the level. But with the stake, or the jackpot, with six zeros at the end of the rainbow, you might feel that you would like a little insurance.

This insurance could be achieved in various forms: a friendly referee, an iron-clad contract for a return match, a secret contract whereby if you lost you were to share a percentage of the new champion's next several fights, or an out-and-out crooked agreement, "We win this time, you win the next."

Shady brokers were wanted for shady deals, and during that decade they were ready-made and to hand in the form of the prohibition gangsters, beer barons, and rum-runners who formed a hidden empire dedicated to slaking the country's illegal thirst.

For at that time of our national lives, we were saddled with one of the most stupid and egregious statutes ever foisted upon weak and sinful human beings, the prohibition law which forbade the purchase and consuming of strong drink, and which resulted in more than three-quarters of the nation not only condoning, but consorting with criminals. So vast was this felonious network, consecrated to procuring us a snort, that it became a government within a government with its own territories, rulers of same, kangaroo courts, laws, and executioners. These lords of the underworld had the power of purchase and the power of terrorism. Prize fighting and prohibition gangsters gravitated toward one another like "H_2" to "O."

Indeed, there was something strangely fascinating about the sudden, big-time boxing of those days which resulted in some truly odd bedfellows. For not only did the illicit beer and liquor magnates boast of owning contracts or pieces of famous fist fighters, but millionaire socialites as well dabbled in this curious form of human merchandising.

The interest of gang lords in acquiring stables of pugs might be said to have begun purely as a sporting hobby and to enhance their personal prestige, a motive not dissimilar from that emanating from the social millionaires, who thus suddenly found themselves getting their names in the papers. What was not surprising was that as overnight, almost, vast sums of money became involved, the already subversive inclinations of the liquor thugs took over. Furthermore, they had just the necessary undercover organizations to handle matters.

While it was highly unlikely that a heavyweight championship fight would be dead fixed for one man to win and the other man to lose, it could and did happen. But since there was usually just too much money at stake to be able wholly to buy out a challenger or a champion, it was when a boy was on the way up that most of the squalid deals were made.

To qualify for a chance at the championship, a fighter had to get himself a record, preferably a string of knockouts, and the fact that his victims were completely unknown made little difference. Thence he progressed to matches with ex-champions or veterans who had seen better days, before finally entering into contention with challengers of similar caliber, or going after a match with the champion himself.

In the rough, old days, compiling such a record was no great problem, since no one paid a great deal of attention to out-of-town fights anyway. Often the first manager to reach the telegraph office won the newspaper decision. But in the post-World War I era, one had to be more careful. A manager bringing a boy along might suddenly, and usually too late, come upon some tough guy among the out-of-town slobs who would flatten his lad and set his career back by at least a year. The way to avoid such an injustice was to invest a little money and bribe the local slobbery to succumb during a certain round from the effects of a violent push to the elbow, or even the breeze stirred up by a near miss. This was known as "the dive," "the Barney," or "going into the tank." And how could you tell, particularly if you were not there?

During my sportswriting days I have seen, I am sure, a number of these fakes perpetrated before my eyes, for the thugs were not shy even of invading Madison Square Garden with some of their make-believe. But even when everything pointed to the fact that the boys were waltzing and that the actual knockout blow would not have discommoded an infant in arms, it was extraordinarily difficult to be absolutely certain. Even the lax American libel laws gave one pause before writing an outright accusation.

There was, however, no lack of ringside innuendo and trade gossip. On many a night one wended one's way to the Garden, the Polo Grounds, or Yankee Stadium, tipped off from various sources, reliable as well as not, that the thing was in the bag for so-and-so. With the game riddled with gamblers, gangsters, small-time punks and crooks hoping to become big-time, jealous managers, and gossipmongers, the chances were the rumors might be true.

There was no way, however, that you could prove it, any more than you could substantiate the existence of secret contracts or that some local referee had been advised what to do if he knew what was good for him and wanted to keep his skin free from unhealthy perforations. Same would be to harass fighter A at every turn, warning him, badgering him, getting in his way, pulling at him and leaning heavily upon him in the clinches, interfering with his in-fighting, while letting fighter B get away with murder. If fighter B was so unfortunate as to be floored, he was to give him the old "One—one-and-a-half—Two—two-and-a-half count until he was able to arise, at which point the referee was then to busy himself for at least thirty seconds cleaning the resin off fighter A's gloves before permitting him to resume, thus giving the boy he was protecting a necessary siesta.

Sometimes this kind of terrorism extended to the buildup circuit, particularly when the boy being built was gangster-owned. And there were known instances of some local lad concerned with his own career and doing very nicely, suddenly between rounds being treated to a glimpse of artillery coyly displayed beneath his corner, following upon which he would lose all interest in the contest and opt for survival over his name in the paper among the recently deceased.

When one went to fight in another city, say Detroit, Pittsburgh or St. Louis, there was always some local thug who let it be known that he was the power and could fix it for you to win or lose, depending upon whether or not you paid. It might be nothing but wind, but who could afford to take a chance? The manager paid. If his boy won, the gangster got the credit, if he lost the manager was usually too scared to ask for his money back, unless he had a coterie of gangsters of his own. From time to time double-crossing parties did wind up wearing concrete overcoats at the bottom of the old mill stream.

In that decade not even the good name of James Joseph Tunney could escape the accusation that he had "protection" in the first Dempsey fight in the shape of a character called Max Boo Boo Hoff.

As a matter of fact, the only umbrella that Tunney needed in Philadelphia that night would have been one to have kept off the rain which pelted down the half hour during which time he was battering Dempsey to a ruin. There was no evidence whatsoever from the handling of the bout that Gene was being favored.

Still, the situation was ripe for just such kind of gossip. Tunney's manager was an old-line, old-time Irishman, Billy Gibson, a veteran of the bad old days, when managers were not above taking out some kind of an insurance policy in a strange city.

For that matter there was rumor about Dempsey being involved in a similar deal, a year later in Chicago. He was then no longer managed by Kearns, but by another old-time shanty Irishman, Leo P. Flynn. Flynn was linked to that name of a name in the Windy City, so potent and violent that no one dared even pronounce it in public but referred to him as Mr. Al Brown in hotel lobbies, elevators, and night clubs. It was none other than the great Capone himself who was said to have spread the mantle of his protection over Dempsey at the time of the second Tunney fight at Soldier Field.

We were all so close to it then; these figures lived, walked, breathed; we saw them with our own eyes. Even we, the sportswriters, seemed to be moving in a mild atmosphere of danger which was both romantic and exciting. It made far better copy and was more fun to believe than not. Now, looking backward over the passage of so many years, much of the accusations, plots, rumors, gossip, threats, and tales appear to have had no more substance than the turbulence in a wind tunnel, and all the promises of protection were probably 99%10 per cent hot air, the kind that big gang leaders love to dispense. In all probability Hoff would have been no more able to "protect" Gene in Philadelphia than Capone was able to exert any genuine influence outside his own organization in Chicago.

On the contrary, if it was true that Flynn had been so stupid as to enter into any kind of alliance with Capone, which I doubt, the mere rumor of it was sufficient to cost Dempsey his chance of winning. For with no more than hearsay of such a connection

FPG

The night they cheered Tunney to the echo—refereeing the International Anglo-American Golden Gloves bouts.

to go by, the Illinois Boxing Commission substituted Referee Dave Barry for Referee Davy Miller, who was supposed to be a "Capone man," and probably wasn't. It was Dave Barry who gave Tunney the famous "long count" and saved his championship. And there was nothing crooked about *that*. It was Dempsey's own fault, as he has admitted hundreds of times since, for not retiring to a neutral corner.

Actually, none of these charges ever really stood up or were tested to a conclusion in court and supported by judgment. And eventually we learned that these gang leaders were as vain and proud of their press cuttings as any movie star, and let their press agents rumor and puff them into allegations of power that had little basis in truth.

There were further accusations rife at the time that, on his way to the top, Tunney had engaged in several fixed fights, notably with characters by the names of Italian Jack Herman, Bartley Madden. A newspaper actually printed a story to the effect that Herman had gone into the tank for Tunney.

I remember asking Gene, point-blank, once if they were true or false. He replied, "Oh, come on, Paul! Why should I have to bother to fix one like that? If I can't knock out all the Italian Jack Hermans there are, one after the other, I'd never put on another glove."

The logic of this was irrefutable, and what is more, from the physical point of view it had to be true. As to why the journal was never sued, it would have been both tactless and senseless for Gibson to have attempted to bring a newspaper into court. It only took a manager to get himself a hint of a reputation as a suer and the press would drop him and his stable like a hot potato.

The fact was that neither Gibson nor Tunney could have bought their way through such competition as Erminio Spalla, Harry Greb, Georges Carpentier, or Tommy Gibbons. Tunney fought his way to the top through the toughest opposition available with no more protection than he was able to provide himself with, using his two hands, his own skill, dexterity, and courage. There was not then, nor is there now, any sense in imagining that the ex-Marine would pursue the most difficult antagonists to establish his right as Dempsey's challenger, beat them or knock them out, and then hire unheard-of or inferior artists to quit to him.

Why then was Tunney dogged by these stories all through his career?

I cannot bring myself to deposit the blame far from the doorstep of the late Bard of Avon. True, there were jealousies and, no doubt, an occasional cabal by rival managers to denigrate Gene and if possible sidetrack him in favor of one of their own fighters. But all through Tunney's rise, one heard over and over the same theme: a bona fide pugilist ought not to be quoting *Hamlet,* or caught browsing in a copy of Spengler's *Decline of the West* in the solitude of a bosky Adirondack dell where his training camps were pitched. There must be something phony about a fellow like that. Such behavior was an offense to the entire industry, and the thing to do was to take this stainless knight down a peg or two. One way to accomplish this was to smear his character.

During all of his ring life, Gene Tunney fought a running battle with the press and in particular the boxing writers who, almost to a man, were arrayed against him, disliked him, and lost no opportunity to pillory him for his bookishness and present him in as bad a light as possible. It is true, from time to time, he looked us straight in the eye with that level, honest gaze and lied to us cheerfully, mostly on matters pertaining to his private life. But why should he be denied decanting a bit of sauce onto the gander, since we often were lying about him, or at least printing stories about him based on no more than rumor and which never had been thoroughly investigated?

Some of us, Pegler and myself included, took an almost perverse joy in hounding this character who, by every tenet and qualification, was the twin of Jack Armstrong, the All-American boy. He had his friends and adherents among the press as well, but it was hard to hear the hosannas for the pounding of the hammers. The great American dream was of the man who could rise above the station to which he was born by his comportment, lending dignity where dignity was lacking and succeeding in the face of all odds. And here we were trying to knock him down. It simply made no sense. But then, neither did much else that happened in that extraordinary decade, and which made Pegler's characterization of it as "The Era of Wonderful Nonsense" so apt.

Still looking backward to my sportswriting days and the pieces I wrote, I am afraid I do not see myself as a very bright boy. In blind and stubborn defense of the Dempsey image, I took sides, picked up the wrong story, and missed out on the far more thrilling one that was being enacted under my nose. This was the stalking of Dempsey for six, long years and the patient, painstaking preparation to defeat him by a man who saw it as the only way to win the right to marry a socialite heiress of the great Carnegie family. I didn't even know he knew her, or had been introduced to her many years before by Sam Pryor, one of the Connecticut scions who liked and admired the young, ex-Marine prize fighter.

In retrospect the stalk is still fascinating. Tunney was at ringside for Dempsey's title defenses against Brennan, Firpo, and Carpentier, analyzing his style; he studied every motion picture available of Jack in action for further evidence of weaknesses; to advance his education, he employed sparring partners whom Dempsey had used; he spent long hours in secret, practicing punches and maneuvers to exploit openings he had learned that Dempsey provided. And lastly, he avoided no opponents and set the final seal upon his standing as a contender when he fought and knocked out Tommy Gibbons, a clever boxer who had previously gone the route with Dempsey.

How clever we were, we who made Dempsey a 2 to 1 favorite over Tunney in Philadelphia the night of September 23, 1926, and how little we knew. And how abysmally we had failed to penetrate the secret of what was really at stake the night that the ex-Marine stepped into the rain-sodden ring. Here was a man who was pitting his future happiness on his skill in an encounter against the most formidable fighter of modern times. He stood to lose everything he ever was or hoped to be. Actually it was this meeting, in which over ten tense rounds Tunney battered one side of the champion's face into a piece of raw and swollen beef and took his title away from him, which was the climax the Three Sisters of Fate had prepared when they tangled the skeins of the lives of the two men.

For this victory was the key that unlocked the vaults of Fort Knox, as it were, for Tunney and made possible his million dollars for the second match with Dempsey in Chicago and a half million more for his last fight with Tommy Heeney, after which he retired and married his heiress.

And what of that famous long count at Chicago, and who was right and who was wrong, and what might have been? I was there, front row, working press, dictating blow by blow through a leased telephone wire to our composing room in New York. Tunney lay crumpled on the canvas in front of me. I looked into his face; he was stunned and glassy-eyed. He never would have made it to his feet before "ten," I'll swear.

There was such pandemonium in the amphitheater that my man at the other end of the line could not hear what I was saying. Above me, Dempsey foolishly was standing over Tunney, unheeding of the referee motioning him to a far corner. How much time elapsed before New York finally heard that Tunney was down, before Dempsey at last obeyed instructions and the count began?

Next to me a little lop-eared man with a bashed-in nose was gazing with bewilderment at a stopwatch he had clicked into action the moment Tunney had hit the deck. "Why," he said, "he's been down for sixteen seconds!" The little man's name was Battling Nelson and his stopwatch did not lie.

Dempsey was paying for his contempt of the rules and Tunney was cashing in on the intelligence for which we had so long castigated him. For it was Gene's hour after hour of *running backward* during his roadwork that enabled him to avoid Dempsey's killing rush for the remainder of that round and so keep his championship.

Yet really all that vast conclave of excitement-seekers remembered of that fight was that they had seen the old Destroying Angel flame once more into his explosive moment of glory in that seventh round, when he caught the agile Fancy Dan Smarty Pants coming off the ropes and clobbered him. Brute

The only prize fighter who ever beat the game, Gene Tunney with his wife, the former Polly Lauder of Greenwich, Connecticut.

Us was again triumphant, even though diddled out of our just desserts.

Well, these were some of the old stories in the old days which thrilled us and embellished the physical struggles of the gloved fights under Marquis of Queensberry rules. There will be other great battles, curious tales, and outside-ring dramas in the days to come, but when and wherever will we again find two such extraordinary characters locked in combat as Jack Dempsey and Gene Tunney, or who will have meant as much to those who followed their conflicts?

The colossus of tennis, William Tatem Tilden 2nd.

CHAPTER **6**

William Tatem Tilden 2nd

(1893–1953)

Of all the changes in the world of sports that took place between the years 1920 and 1930 none was more astonishing or unpredictable than the emergence of lawn tennis as a spectator game and prime box office attraction.

For it was during that magic decade that the once-despised, girlish, and privately practiced game of tennis became a part of the exaggerated bonanza of those years, was compelled to build its own stadium and cast up upon the scene heroes and heroines who, through their skills and individualities, elevated the gates into the million-dollar class.

However, there are two prior dates to be noted which were of the greatest significance to this extraordinary flowering—1912 and 1913.

It was during the former that a young red-headed Californian of no particular social standing came out of the West to bludgeon his way through the up-to-that-time effete, sparsely attended, and hardly noticed tournaments of the East. He produced a slashing, smashing, whirlwind, attacking game of such speed and power that he swept the Eastern practitioners practically off their courts and raised the eyebrows of the lifted pinkie set right up into their hatbands. His name was Maurice McLoughlin, and the excitement and novelty of his play drew the first real audiences to these matches and actually struck the initial blow which was to free the game forever from the stigmas imposed upon it by its supposedly effeminate nature.

McLoughlin, however, perhaps unfortunately for him, was ahead of his time; the pioneer who retired before he was able to reap the full rewards heaped upon his successors.

In 1913, a mixed doubles team consisting of Miss Mary K. Browne and William T. Tilden 2nd appeared in the East and won the outdoor national championship in that event and a long, lean shadow was cast ahead. For it was the first time the name of Tilden achieved national prominence. But it was not until seven years later, in 1920, when he won the men's outdoor national singles championship and then repeated for five successive years, that this sport came into its own.

This generation, the young people of today, can have no conception of the handicaps which the modern, taxing, violent, and wholly manly game of lawn tennis had to overcome to reach acceptance, and if you can spare a moment from the story of the man chiefly responsible for this change, I will try to give you an idea.

When I was growing up in New York, in the vicinity of Park Avenue and Sixtieth Street, say around 1906 (Park Avenue at that time was an open cut through which the New York Central ran, belching smoke and soot into the neighborhood curtains), I had a friend whose parents, when he was naughty, punished him by dressing him up in girl's clothes for the day.

This, of course, was before the advent of Professor Freud. I never found out whether this popping of their son and heir into drag was their own sublimated wish for a daughter, nor am I able to tell you the result it had upon the unfortunate boy in later life. But I am prepared to say that psychologically the punishment was characteristic of the times.

There was no greater humiliation to which a youth could be exposed than to be made into a girl, or even thought of in that connection by his fellows. At that age I had never heard of such a thing as a homosexual, neither had my colleagues, but the smile-when-you-say-that-word among us was "sissy." When you were called that, you either put up your dukes and battled, or were forever labeled.

And I remember, too, that in our section it was worth your life to be caught walking anywhere east of Lexington Avenue carrying a tennis racquet under your arm. And as for being clad in a pair of ice cream pants and blazer, this was sheerest suicide.

At the turn of the century you had only to be seen in any tough neighborhood bearing one of those bats thus accoutered, to bring out a swarm of young hoodlums, tagging one with mocking, falsetto shrieks of "Deuce, darling" or "Forty-love, dear." Whoever, in the early days of the invention of modern tennis in Great Britain around 1873, substituted the word "love" for the more sensible one of "nought" or "zero" to indicate "no score," imposed a staggering handicap upon it and was responsible, at least in the U.S.A., for a lot of black eyes and bloody noses.

Another encumbrance to a pastime which today is a symbol not only of skill and virility, but toughness and endurance as well (there are few sports more exhausting than a big-time five-set tennis match) was the juxtaposition of the word "lawn." There was nothing the matter with the word "tennis" itself, one of the most ancient games derived from the courts of the Kings of France. Nor was there anything inherently upsetting in "lawn," a patch of grass connected with country or suburban houses which seemed to call for unending mowing and watering.

But put the two together to make "lawn tennis" and at once there arose a vision of prissy dudes in white flannel trousers, prancing about a greensward at Southampton, Newport, Bar Harbor, or Seabright, pitter-patting a ball across a sagging net to young ladies clad in long skirts, puff sleeves, and Gibson Girl hats. Serves were delivered underhand, and such a thing as an overhead kill, net play, or driving the ball straight for the refined countenance of your opponent would have brought shrieks of protest and, no doubt, expulsion from the club. It called up pictures of other cookie-pushers wearing chic, striped blazers and straw boaters with colored college headbands, idling on the sidelines, sipping tea with elegantly lifted pinkies, all on a summer's day. The whole business made for mockery.

Even as late as 1916 and 1917, when I made my first appearances as candidate for the Columbia University crew, I remember the stern warnings issued by our rough, tough, Canadian-born coach, the late Jim Rice, "Don't let me catch any of you fellows going out and playing that there long penis game." For on the crew we were supposed to be men and tennis was even then not considered for a man.

And one of the weirdest ironies in perhaps the entire history

The Tilden projection: dramatist, actor, hero.

. . . and sometimes martyr. Tilden didn't like to lose.

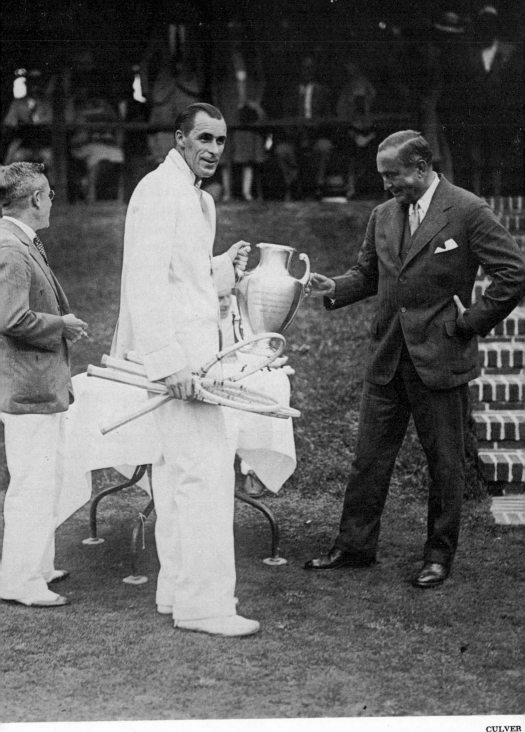

This was the third act curtain called for by the script.

of modern sport is that the personality chiefly responsible for the metamorphosis of tennis from a game looked upon as effeminate to its present-day acceptance was himself, as he so honestly and tragically acknowledged in his own biography, a deviate.

Of all the colorful champions of that era, this man was far and away the oddest fish. As a player he dominated the decade at a period when there were more stars, national or international, to challenge him than ever before or since. As a box office attraction both amateur and professional, he lifted the gate from peanuts into the million-dollar class. As a person he was as strange, independent, and controversial a figure as ever strutted across the sports scene.

He was a colossus! He was a tremendous athlete of unparalleled skill and inexhaustible endurance. And he was 100 per cent ham.

It is astonishing how frequently the characters in this book did not look like athletes, and it applies again to Bill Tilden. He stood six feet, one inch in his tennis socks and never weighed more than 165 pounds. He was built, if you saw him stripped in the locker room, along the lines of a gibbon—the wide shoulders which always seemed somewhat hunched, long, prehensile arms, flat, narrow waist and thin, caliper-like legs. His hair tended to sparseness on top, and he had a long nose and curiously heavy and prognathous jaw. But if you were designing a creature especially for the playing of big-league tennis, you could hardly improve upon Tilden's conformation—the elongated legs for covering the court in giant strides and the powerful shoulders and whiplash arms and wrists for flailing the ball.

Add to this one of the keenest game-analyzing brains of any of the champions, lightning reactions, the temperament of a prima donna, and his own personal tragedy of homosexuality, and one has little difficulty in regarding him as surely a most remarkable character.

At this time in our own development as a nation and a people emerging from war, our heated imaginations and the change from the excitement to the calmer days of peace necessitated the invention of different kinds of daily thrills. To provide these our sports heroes became *personae dramatis* of the great sports sagas. But Tilden was also his own dramatist.

Whereas fate and circumstances, and often the cagey manipulations of astute promoters, cast this or that famous sportsman as hero, heavy, or supporting role, Tilden wrote his own scripts. A total exhibitionist, stage-struck—he chewed up scenery in plays as a member of a number of road companies in the legitimate theater—he could not bear to be anything less than the leading man; Bayard, Cyrano, Galahad, Roland, d'Artagnan all lumped into one. If the spotlight ever wandered from him during his play on the tennis courts, he very quickly pulled it back onto himself. No top-dog or villain parts for Tilden; the sympathy of the audience had to be with him at all times.

You could almost always bet on the graph of the American public following the rise of any champion to his crown. Up and up and up it went with him, in pursuit of his fortunes until he reached the peak and then down it would plunge. Now that he was champ his fickle fans could hardly wait to see him knocked off. This should have been doubly operative in the case of Tilden, for he was not only outstanding and for a time unbeatable, but arrogant, with irritating court mannerisms, disputatious and supercilious. Yet, practically for all of his reign he had the crowd with him.

He achieved this by the very simple and rarely varying drama of the great master teetering on the brink of downfall or even a rout, then rallying and in a superb display of courage, stamina, and often incredible shot-making, snatching victory from what we liked to refer to as the jaws of defeat.

And how Tilden could teeter. If his antagonist could not produce the attack to make him temporarily look bad, or in danger —and there were plenty who could—Tilden would let down, appear off form, or develop a slight injury to handicap himself, until finally there he was, a lone and gallant figure on the courts, staring repulse in the face.

This was not crudely done, but deftly and subtly (Tilden could also throw a point to an opponent blatantly to show his contempt for a linesman's call, and reveal himself as one disdaining to accept an advantage he felt he had not earned)—and so skillfully that we were not conscious of anything but a champion momentarily off stride, until one looked at the score sheet and saw that he was five games down, set point against him, and in danger of blowing the tournament. And then the fun began.

But there was far more to it than just this kind of corny crowd appeal. The man did stir the emotions exactly as great actors do upon the stage, for at tennis he was more than just a champion and a top-notch technician, he was a genius and a superb artist. It was to this artistry that all of us inevitably reacted. It overcame every one of his handicaps, his little tantrums and gestures of pique, sulks, pets, glares, and *moues* and, believe it or not, cries of "Oh, sugar!" when he missed one. They simply did not matter in the light of the heights to which he was able to rise when he wished, or needed to, and in rising would sweep us all out of ourselves and along with him.

It was, as noted, one of the maddest paradoxes of the age that the man who was responsible for bringing about acceptance of tennis as one of the most virile of men's competitive games was effeminate in his mannerisms and behavior. The paradox continued to hold good in that it didn't seem to matter, was hardly noticeable and rarely discussed. And I must confess that during the days I was covering Tilden's matches and writing about him, I didn't even know it, or think about it. His artistry was such that this was all one saw.

For if his personality was doubtful on the male side, his tennis was not. It was as hard, manly, and slashing a game as was ever seen on any court, and all the kids wanted to play and win like Tilden. His image was enormous, an international giant holding off the world. At his peak he beat the Americans, the British, the French, the Japanese, and the Australians. He was invincible *us*.

His strength was as the strength of ten, his blinding service unreturnable, his stamina inexhaustible, and his courage unquestionable. Then how could he be effeminate as well? There was no understanding whatsoever of homosexuality in America forty or fifty years ago. It was either an undercover whisper, or a dirty joke. It was not until World War II that the presence of some during Commando raids revealed that they could be among the cruelest, bravest, and toughest of men.

From the moment Tilden stepped onto the grass court, he dominated the scene to such an extent that there was no room in one's head for anything but the drama that was about to be unfolded.

He did it with a tennis racquet, an oval bat strung with catgut, but it might have been a sword, a gun, a bow, or even a conductor's baton. It was not only the implement of the game, it was his instrument of creation. With it he could make us feel sad, thrilled, glad, worried, anxious, relieved, and even ecstatic, any mood that he desired to arouse; and frightened, too, for believe me the man was tough and the killer instinct was there when called upon, as brutal as that in any fighter or football player. To his opponents it was a contest; with Tilden it was an expression of his own tremendous and overweening ego, coupled with feminine vanity.

To this extraordinary spiritual, emotional, and intellectual approach Tilden brought unusual physical mastery and technical skill. Like all great champions he was a student of every facet of his sport, a man with the interest and curiosity to pry into everything that had to do with producing winning tennis.

Lawn tennis as it had developed, from the time of Maurice McLoughlin, is a game of mathematics and angles, just as, let us say, baseball is one of timing and judgment. Each calls for different equipment and the participants become dexterous in their use. But these play no more than a mechanical part in the basic concept of the pastime. With ball and bat, problems of judgment are created and the race is against time: man arriving at base that split second before the throw. With the tennis racquet, the speed of flight of the properly hit ball, and the arbitrary confines of the court, angles are created which decide a point one way or another, either by forcing a bad return or setting the opponent the problem impossible of solution: i.e., the passing shot. But angles are mathematics, and Tilden was the master tennis mathematician.

The average player has to think about the components of making a proper shot, just as the average week-end golfer is not bothered about where he will hit the ball, but whether he will hit it at all, and how far and how straight. Players of modern tournament tennis, however, have their technique so perfected that their racquets are merely an implementation of their thoughts and strategic plans. Tilden had the stroke to meet every type of attack and the legs to get him to the spot for handling it. In aggression he was wholly formidable with a forehand and backhand drive which, for power hitting, have rarely been equaled, a booming cannon-ball service, cunning volley, and a smashing net game when he wanted to move up there. Further, he had the ability to turn what seemed like impossible gets, with his opponent already congratulating himself, into winning placements.

He was the perfect player and, as a result of this perfection, he won the American National Turf Court Championship seven times, the Wimbledon title three times, shared in the U.S. doubles five times (between 1918 and 1927), and in Davis Cup matches between 1920 and 1930 won seventeen and lost only five singles matches and shared in four doubles victories. From 1920 through 1929 inclusive, Tilden was ranked first in the U.S.A.

The difficulties in which Tilden often found himself embroiled during this brilliant period arose from the fact that he was not a snob, nor a socialite, nor a Mainliner. He came from a middle-class Philadelphia merchant family. And tennis was then still a snob game.

But there are snobs and snobs. The original tennis fathers (and moms) were ladies and gentlemen who did not look down upon those who did not play tennis. They were pleased with their own society and probably did not bother to look down at all.

But there were a great number of Americans shortly before and after World War I who were looking upward and dying to break into the closed circle of the charmed Four Hundred. The game of tennis was a means of entry to some, and those were the genuine copper-plated, triple-riveted, gold-rimmed snobs.

These were the new rich, the climbers and the pseudo-socialites who later were all lumped under the general heading of Cafe Society, and who thought that joining a tennis club would bestow upon them a large part of the standing they sought. The characteristics of the members of this class and their idea of comporting themselves in the manner of the *crème de la crème* was rudeness, arbitrary bullheadedness, and stuffed-shirtism. Quietly, control of the game passed into their hands as the genuine aristocracy abandoned tennis in favor of polo, a pastime that demanded even more money and more space to be enjoyed. Their hero was Tommy Hitchcock and surrounding him was a crowd of tough, hard-drinking, well-mannered men. The Long Island polo set was authentic, but by this time the tennis crowd was as phony as a dime-store engagement ring.

How did the tennis snobs manage to keep their clammy hands upon the sport just as it was bursting from its chrysalis, ready for flight to its place in the sun? They were simply there. They ran the clubs, they had the only courts and the stadia and thus were able to promote and hold the big tournaments.

They formed the backbone of the U. S. Lawn Tennis Association of forty years ago, stiffened by a few leftover antediluvian stuffed shirts of the previous generation. These climbers not only had no background for manners and genteel behavior themselves, but often by their conduct and superior airs succeeded in making amateur or assistant snobs out of many of the girls and boys who were attracted to the game.

The sudden shower of sports shekels of the twenties sent a shiver of surprise, shock, and joy down the spines of the members of the committees of the important tennis clubs. After years when tennis was only a pay-out pastime, draining funds for upkeep of courts and damage to the locker rooms perpetrated by soused members, now, out of the blue, it was big box office.

And what was most marvelous, it was theirs, all theirs, and for free—well, almost for free. Theoretically the big money drawers were all amateurs who were not supposed to get a penny for their services beyond a cup that in those days could wholesale for $49.98.

With sell-out houses for the national championships, Davis and Wightman Cup matches and other invitation attractions, you can understand the anxiety of everyone connected with lawn tennis that the players should not sully their amateur standing by becoming a party to the transfer of hard cash. It was this attitude that so irritated Tilden and made him the gadfly of the U.S.L.T.A. It was not so much the money involved but the impudence of the Association's approach.

For three-quarters of a century now, the United States has been dogged by the amateur problem and all of the hypocrisy connected with it. But it really took the Russians and their simple, uncomplicated attitude to sports to show up the utter ridiculousness of our interpretation of an amateur versus a professional in modern times.

From 1920 to 1930 it was tennis which provided the most strident battleground raised by this question, with foot running, golf, and college football adding to the confusion as soon as they joined the big money earners.

Class-conscious Britain in the 1800s invented the distinction between the amateur and the professional and it was a simple one. The amateur was a gentleman and the professional wasn't. When the gentlemen consented to risk soiling their hands by meeting the professionals in a cricket match, the latter entered the clubhouse by the back door and through the kitchen. There was no financial problem connected at the beginning, since a gentleman did not make money; he *had* money. In modern times who is, or isn't a gentleman has become just as confused as to who is, or who isn't an amateur.

As social circles began to widen, so did these distinctions, and the dollar offered a convenient dividing line. A fellow who in any way, shape, form, or manner permitted his connection with sport to be associated with the long green, was lumped as a professional, even if he had no more than sold sweat bands or tennis socks over the counter in a sporting goods shop during the Christmas holidays. An amateur played only for fun and recreation and was rich enough not to have to worry where his next dollar was coming from.

The trouble was that when an amateur sport, such as tennis, became big business, it was discovered that this type of simon-pure was unfortunately in very short supply.

When American tennis passed into the Golden Decade and the West Side Tennis Club-Forest Hills Stadium phase, what the U. S. Lawn Tennis Association required was amateur tennis players whose game reached professional standards. To acquire such proficiency meant they would have to devote practically all their time not only to practicing, but traveling on the tennis circuit and playing in tournaments the year round to keep sharp.

Their services, of course, were to be donated for free and under no circumstances were they to demand any part of the huge gates that their box-office personalities were attracting. They were to maintain themselves and be satisfied with travel and subsistence allowances about on a par with those given to a soldier or sailor.

Technically they got them, but from that moment on, of course, the genuine tennis amateur was as extinct as the dodo and everyone connected with the game, or who profited by it with the exception of the ball boys, was as crooked as the proverbial corkscrew, in the ethical if not the physical sense as well.

Many of the so-called amateurs were compelled to cheat in order to keep going, that is to say, take money under the table, and the phrase "tennis bum" joined the American language. The officials knew they were cheating, but closed their eyes to it, otherwise there would not have been any stars to tone up the box office. As long as the cheating remained under cover, it was condoned. But let a player turn honest enough to try to make a few pennies with either personal or ghost-written newspaper articles, or a temporary job with a sporting goods house, and he was immediately disbarred and banished into outer darkness, unless, as will be seen, his need was so great that the officials were compelled to backtrack on their own ruling and reinstate him.

If crooked seems a strong word to use in this context it is because there are simply no shades between honesty and twisting. A man cannot be a slight thief; he is or he isn't. And the absurd amateur rule and the constructions put upon it made dishonest men of everyone connected with amateur sport. This covers the ruling bodies of track meets, college football, golf, college baseball, or any other recreation in which amateurs were responsible for large gate receipts and where eye-closing was involved. It took only the merest droop of the eyelid and the whole affair was not on the level any more. It was in this atmosphere that an entire generation of young athletes grew up with a very early introduction to the double standard.

Where this state of affairs touched William Tatem Tilden 2nd

BROWN BROTHERS

CULVER

WIDE WORLD

was the fact that he was no baby, but an intelligent, educated, sensitive man and hence a perpetual rebel against the hypocrisy of this system.

As well as their greatest star and box office attraction he was also the *enfant terrible* of the Lawn Tennis Association. Into this setup he fitted just like a hysterical bull in a china shop. An anti-snob, he hated their guts, fought with them, ridiculed them, and rammed his weird personality down their throats for ten years. The great god Mazuma reigned and Bill Tilden was his profit. For this reason they had to put up with his mannerisms, umpire-baiting, refusal to conform, and an occasional shrewish offensiveness that matched their own. Tilden didn't give a damn for anyone or anything but the game and his own image.

Tilden's battles with the tennis greats of his era—Little Bill Johnston, Vinny Richards, Dick Williams, Lacoste, Cochet, Borotra, Manuel Alonso from Spain, Patterson and Norman Brooks from Australia, Shimizu and Ichiya Kumagae from Japan, during those years were classics and, in the decade, drew more than a million dollars through the turnstiles. But they were mild compared to his rows with the Lawn Tennis Association which, at one time in 1928, reached the peak of international incident.

At that time the Davis Cup Committee of the U. S. Lawn Tennis Association had discovered that Tilden had been picking up some loose change for writing newspaper articles while traveling abroad. The idea of an amateur laying his hands on some cash into which the tennis body could not get its hooks was so depressing that Tilden was promptly suspended and barred from further amateur play.

But hold, the suspension came just at the time that Big Bill was due to meet the French Davis Cup team at Roland Garros Stadium in Paris, in the challenge round of the international competition.

The stadium was sold out, the French amateur body likewise being no dopes at cashing in, but the big attraction was, naturally, *le Grand Guillaume*. With Tilden blacklisted, a lot of people were going to ask for their money back. The French screamed loud and long. It was Tilden or else, if the two countries were to remain on the footing inaugurated by the Marquis de Lafayette. Myron T. Herrick, the United States Ambassador to France, was compelled to telephone the chairman of the Davis Cup Committee in the United States to say that Tilden must be reinstated for the sake of international amity.

Sweetly cooperative at this point, the Committee, which had barred Tilden as a professional, waved its wand over Big William and metamorphosed him back into an amateur once more for the Davis Cup matches in France. But, immediately upon his return to the United States, they magicked him back again into a professional and banned him from taking part in the United States singles championship. The French won the Davis Cup that year by four matches to one, which may have had something to do with this waspish revenge, which was only exceeded in 1930 when, after Tilden won the world's championship at Wimbledon, the Committee completely ignored him in its national ranking on the basis of a rumor that he was about to turn professional. And no single player ever did more for the U.S.L.T.A. than William Tatem Tilden 2nd. In the meantime, lesser stars were picking up five hundred dollars at a clip for appearing at invitation tournaments at home and abroad, as well as their traveling tickets and more than generous expenses. The custom at that time was to collect total travel expenses from each tournament. When added up this made a nice little income. It was this kind of condoned dishonesty which was anathema to Tilden.

As a professional, Tilden racked up an even more amazing record than as an amateur, for he was thirty-eight when he relinquished his amateur status, and from 1931 through 1935 he compiled 340 wins to 147 losses, against such competition as Kozeluh, Nusslein, Richards, Hunter, Cochet, and Vines.

When he finished as an active professional player, Tilden's love for the game, a love far more generous and enduring than that of any tennis committee man, manifested itself in his teaching of the young, until the unfortunate deviate tragedy that brought his life tumbling down about his ears in 1946 and sent him to jail. He never really managed to fight his way back before his untimely death at the age of sixty in 1953.

But those of us who covered his matches between 1920 and 1929 and sat spellbound in the press marquee at the West Side Tennis Club's Forest Hills Stadium, on Long Island, or at the Germantown Cricket Club, outside Philadelphia, will remember him only as the great actor-dramatist, standing on the base line, pausing until every eye was on him and every lip stilled, to coil, uncoil, and release his thunder-and-lightning service, *obligato* to the theme of the ever-recurring melodrama, "Tilden Wins Again."

Knute Rockne, the coach with a difference.

CHAPTER **7**

Knute Rockne

(1888–1931)

If you are interested in the passage of time and the changes it brings about, you have only to glance at the photographs of the football teams of the 1900s and those of today and, if nothing else, note the difference in attire and armor plating.

Our forefather, his hair neatly parted in the middle, wore short pants known as "moleskins," either quilted or with some sort of ribbed stiffening in them, a woolen jersey, and over it a kind of leather jerkin. Underneath was a device of leather called schimmels, that laced across the shoulders, to protect the collarbone from breakage. The helmet, if and when worn, was of soft leather and covered the ears. Some players used a rubber noseguard.

Compare this mild sort of padding with the almost rigid armor worn today and in particular the solid, rock-hard, plastic helmet with its steel projections.

The uniforms have altered, as have the size and shape of the ball, and the rules of the game itself have been changed incessantly, to the point where a veteran of the year 1900 might not understand the play of 1965 unless an interpreter were at hand to explain it to him.

It was during that famous decade of 1920 to 1930 that football underwent possibly its greatest transition from old-fashioned to modern.

But it was also during that period that a brand-new phenomenon appeared in American football and one which has all but disappeared today. It developed a nationwide emotion that before the decade was out had become almost religious in its nature, and Knute Rockne was its high priest.

At this extraordinary time in the history of American sports as well as that of the people of the United States, Knute Kenneth Rockne, football coach of Notre Dame, was himself a most prodigious, phenomenal, and singular person and more than any other, directly responsible for the extent and violence of the spirit that infected the game and spread to the farthest corners of the country. For ten years this bald, round-faced man with the squashed-in nose and his sensational teams, each fall, initiated a six-week emotional binge among fans, but particularly involving heretofore non-fans of the game of football, that amounted almost to the hysteria of evangelism.

Prior to this, football player Joe College was something of a comic figure with his turtle-necked sweater, Buster Brown haircut, flying wedge, and determination, if need be, to "Die for dear old Rutgers," to the accompaniment of a chant of "Rah-Rah-Rah, Sis Boom Ah" from the crowd on the sidelines, to stimulate him to the sacrifice. Mass cheering has survived in modern football, but it is today nothing but a spectator catharsis and is considered a nuisance by the player who has business to get on with and signals of logarithmic complication to remember and transmit in the pre-play huddles.

Early interest centered around the Big Three, the Universities of Yale, Princeton, and Harvard, but the crowds attending their annual titanic clashes were composed of alumni and their families. Considering the enrollment of these universities, graduating hundreds of nubile young men every year, it did not take long for them to breed pennant-waving partisan and vociferous audiences for these contests. There might be a few outsiders, ambitious youngsters of the ever-increasing middle class, who hoped someday to attain university status, who were "for" Yale, or "for" Harvard, but by and large the rivalries between these great seats of learning were family affairs.

Newspapers in the East were beginning to give publicity to the annual games involving the three, since many of their readers were connected in one way or another as partisans of the universities. Socially the Big Game was a wonderfully gay and youthful affair, featuring the prettiest girls in the world decked out in chrysanthemums and bright ribbons, accompanied by

handsome, coonskin-coated young men, bearing pennants showing the names and colors of the universities and with flasks on
their hips since Prohibition was with us. These clashes often coin-
cided with the Thanksgiving festival; November winds brought
carmine to fresh, young faces; young hearts, particularly feminine ones, beat high, and on the field below, twenty-two heroes
patriotically and chivalrously battled for the glory of alma mater
and the admiring glances of the little beauties in the stands.

The man in the street, however, largely ignored it. The hullabaloo struck him as juvenile, the game of football itself as faintly
ridiculous, with its pushing and shoving and piling up, and there
was still largely the situation of town and gown; the self-made
man versus the college smartie. It was Knute Rockne, in the
main, who brought about a drastic change in the situation.

Neither a born American nor an Irishman, nor a Catholic, until toward the end of his life he became a convert, he was the
coach of the University of Notre Dame, located at South Bend,
Indiana; a Catholic university and a stronghold of Irish Catholi-
cism in the Middle West. It was the semi-religious background
of this school which lent just that touch of mysticism and emo-
tionalism as a starter. But all the rest of the extraordinary spirit
and hysteria which marked so many of the games played by
Notre Dame during that decade were supplied by Rockne.

The sentimental jag reached its high point in the month of
October before, during, and after the annual contest between
Notre Dame and the cadets of the United States Military Academy at West Point, played in New York City; an affair which
took on almost the quality of a pagan autumnal rite, and engaged the passionate observation of millions of people.

You will see if you look at photographs of the early Notre
Dame teams which first came to New York, that their costumes
and headgear are old-fashioned, somewhat between the earliest
uniforms and the modern. But there is something equally old-
fashioned belonging to that era of the twenties that doesn't
show up in pictures. It is the aura of dedication that was quite
different from anything one seems to feel or experience about
football and its participants now, except perhaps, curiously
enough, in the ranks of the professionals and their adherents. It

The young Rockne.   *The old fox.*

is the pros and their fans who, by and large, have taken over the
fervency that used to attend the college games.

That difference, I am convinced, was supplied by one man,
this same Knute Rockne, himself a football star of Notre Dame
from 1911 through 1913 and head coach at the university from
1919 until his tragic death in an airplane crash in the West in
1931.

He was a hired hand, engaged like so many others to teach
the sport to university students, train and advise them, prepare

them physically as well as spiritually and strategically and turn
out winning teams if possible. But more than any other in his
profession he captured the hearts and imaginations of the Americans of his time.

He was responsible for many strategic innovations in football
play, such as the shift and dramatic use of the forward pass that
opened up the attack and made it more visual. But it was for
quite a different contribution that he made his major impact
upon both his day and the game.

He brought an extra dimension to football and in particular
to the teams he coached, which enabled the spectators to share
in the emotions engendered by the struggle on the field far more
than they had ever done before.

American college football was a battle which very often tran-
scended not only itself but those participating in it as well, to
the point where suddenly the onlooker saw it no longer as a
spectacle provided by two sets of young men, but rather as a
giant and abstract manifestation of two contending wills. If offered a phase of the classic physics paradox of what happens
when an unstoppable force encounters an immovable object.

Further, unlike other sports, there were no villains in these
college clashes. The teams were too ephemeral, here one year,
graduated the next. Partisanship was a matter of adherence to
a university rather than individual members of its football
squads. Outstanding stars achieved tremendous followings, but
whoever heard of hating a halfback or an end?

And finally, there was another kind of sharing for which
Knute Rockne was responsible, since it was his teams that sent
the renown and name of Notre Dame soaring. It took the form
of the famous assistant Irish and Subway Alumni of the South
Bend institution, whose headquarters were in New York, but
whose members were scattered to the four corners of the land
wherever there was anyone named Ryan or Rafferty, Clancy or
O'Houlahan; or Kraus or Cohen or Tony Bacigalupo.

This was quite one of the most amazing phenomena and
transitions of the times. Suddenly everybody wanted to get into
the act and belong. Hundreds of thousands of people prior to
this time who had looked down upon the game as "Rah-Rah"

stuff now wanted to identify themselves with it, an identification, incidentally, far more rabid and partisan even than that exhibited by the alumni, or family members of universities.

Dates and facts here become a matter of some importance. The initial Army-Notre Dame meeting took place at West Point in the fall of 1913. Up to that time few had ever known Notre Dame in the East. The Westerners won 35 to 13 and from then on one heard plenty about the Catholic school.

One of the players on the Notre Dame team of that year was an end by the name of Rockne, another was a young back, Gus Dorais. The Notre Dame coach was Jesse Harper. For the first time experts in the East saw the forward pass—mostly Dorais to Rockne, used as a part of sustained offensive football rather than a last-minute desperation. Overnight it seemed that the game had been opened up, revolutionized, and turned into a thrilling and dramatic spectacle, no longer dependent upon partisan loyalties for thrills. It had become something to watch. But the Subway Alumni were not yet.

In 1919, the year when Knute Rockne was appointed head coach at Notre Dame, and subsequently in 1920 and 1921, his teams were Western champions and national champions winning a total of twenty-eight games and losing one.

From 1920 through 1930, Notre Dame won ninety-six, lost twelve, and was tied three times.

The man behind this fantastic string of victories was this same Rockne, and West Point and Notre Dame acquired the greatest rooting sections in the history of the game. Only seventy thousand at a time could crowd into Yankee Stadium in New York actually to see them play, but millions became fanatical adherents via the radio and the newspapers. The game of football —at least this particular one involving Army and Notre Dame— had broken through every class barrier that still existed in the United States.

World War I had supplied a new and ready-made cheering section for the two service teams. If during our brief embroilment in that catastrophe you had worn khaki, you were for Army; if bell-bottomed trousers, Navy was your team from then on. The annual clash between Army and Navy took on an importance it never had before, far transcending even the game between Yale and Harvard, for now we had alumni, if not actually of West Point or the Naval Academy, at least of the two services. But until the advent of Notre Dame there was no school which extended a mass appeal to ordinary civilians.

With the sky-rocketing of this university out of the West, their brand of exciting, razzle-dazzle, wide-open football, the wonderful sobriquet of "Fighting Irish" pinned on them by the sports-writers (in spite of the fact that the majority of the names of the team members were not Irish—of the thirty letter-winners in 1927, for instance, only seven could be said to have monickers stemming from the Ould Sod), everything changed. The warm affection and the curious kind of sports love engendered by the unique personality of Rockne led literally millions of people who had never been to college or seen a campus to adopt Notre Dame as their very own and thereafter identify themselves with the school.

Beginning with 1923, New Yorkers had the opportunity of seeing this team in action, provided they could buy their way into the baseball parks. That year the Army-Notre Dame tussle was played at Ebbets Field in Brooklyn. In 1924 and 1925, fifty-five thousand souls jammed the Polo Grounds beneath Coogan's

He joined in the drills . . .

WORLD

Bluff. From then on it was seventy thousand persons packing every nook and cranny of Yankee Stadium.

New York was never before, or since, so sweetly gay and electric as it was when Rock brought his boys to town; the city was wild with excitement and filled with pretty girls and gray-clad cadets who thronged the hotel ballrooms when it was over, while the civilian fans argued or battled it out in the Third Avenue speakeasies.

These Interborough Rapid Transit Notre Damers came from every walk of life; Gentile and Jew, Broadway show-biz and nightclub dolls, bartenders, prize fighters, cab drivers, book-makers, delicatessen store owners, denizens of the half as well as the whole underworld, rich man, poor man, beggarman, thief —and, of course, the Irish.

For a nickel train ride, a scalper's price of admission, and two bits more for a feather, or a banner, they became faithful and fervent rooters. They felt that they belonged, and that the won-derful bizarre and romantic mantle of Irishness was spread over them. A large portion of them were no more genuine Hibernians than were those members of the Notre Dame squads whose names ended in "ski," "berger," "isch," or "vitch," but it made no difference to the self-appointed alumni. Once they had decked themselves out in the Notre Dame colors, predominantly green, naturally, their identities were merged with those ex-traordinary football wizards from the West.

The very fact that this squad came from that part of the country and the never-before-heard-of town of South Bend, lent added mystery and fascination. There were some pretty good football players and teams around the East at that time too: Syracuse, Colgate, Cornell, Pennsylvania, not to mention the Big Three, Princeton, Harvard, and Yale, as the game developed. But when the brilliant and winning "Irish" arrived, the masses ignored the local squads, allied themselves with the strangers, and took them to its collective heart. In the mongrel mixture of the melting pot, all became Irish and "Fighting Irish" as well.

When the November sun had set behind the Polo Grounds or Yankee Stadium, and the Notre Dame eleven had quit the gridiron with the football and the winning score, it would be

these same bartenders, bookmakers, shopkeepers, nightclub door-
men, and Broadway bums who would flood onto the field and
begin rocking the goalposts to bring them down, cart them off,
and carve them up into souvenir splinters to be carried thereafter as talismans of the luck of the Irish.

One famous backfield of those days was most felicitously
named "The Four Horsemen" by star sportswriter and poet the
late Grantland Rice. He took the name from the Ibanez novel and
moving picture: the Four Horsemen of biblical lore, Famine,
Pestilence, Destruction, and Death, and this kind of publicity
and dramatic buildup was on a par with that which was greet-
ing heroes and millionaires in other big-league sports. Cash began to flow into the coffers of university athletic associations as
never before.

But if, as noted, players were somewhat ephemeral—three
years saw them graduated and replaced by others—one gigantic
figure remained, the high priest of those football days and the
idol of not only small boys, but adults as well, and that was
Rockne himself. He had magnetism to burn and that indefinable
champion's touch, that intangible something that inspired not
only his players, but reached beyond them to the lowliest self-
appointed Subway Alumnus who loved and rooted for "Kanute
Rockne of Noter Dame's Fightin' Irish." Dempsey had it, Tunney
had it; so had Johnny Weissmuller, Tommy Hitchcock, Earl
Sande, Bobby Jones, the Babe, Red Grange, champions all.
When they came into a room, you knew they were there.
Wherever and whenever Rockne appeared there was no doubt
as to who was the star of the show.

Since this is not a biography of Rockne but only an estimate
of his influence on his times, it will suffice to remind you that
he came to the United States as a boy of five in 1893 with his
immigrant Norwegian family which made its home on Chicago's
northwest side in the Logan Square area, populated mainly by
Irish and Swedes, and here his Americanization commenced. It
progressed via the American love of sports through sandlot football, baseball, and track; grammar school and high school, to the
halls of Notre Dame—then an unpretentious Catholic school
where young Rockne opted to go instead of to the University of

. . . and showed them how . . .

Illinois, because he would be able to work his way through, and the one thousand dollars he had saved at odd jobs to pay his way would go farther.

There were many other great football teachers in that era, contemporary with him: Pop Warner, Hurry-Up Yost, Amos Alonzo Stagg, and Percy Haughton, but none of them had that extra, star quality that Knute possessed and the ability so to fuse eleven men into a unit representative of his own peculiar and often impish spirit. His teams sometimes played football that had a definite tinge of humor, because Rockne was a gay, witty man, and made his practice sessions light-hearted and enjoyable. And this, too, managed to communicate itself to us.

Coaches are often overrated. After all, it is the boys who get out onto the field, take the knocks, and carry the ball. But every so often a genuine colossus appears whose influence and teaching cannot be underestimated, and Rockne towered head and shoulders over the best of his profession. He took four of the worst freshman bumblers ever seen falling over their own feet, or running into one another—Miller, Layden, Stuhldreher, and Crowley—a quartet of totally different characters and temperament, and within a year welded them into the greatest back-

field combination ever seen on a football gridiron up to that
time. These were Grantland Rice's famous "Four Horsemen" who
flourished in 1922, 1923, and 1924 to tie Army once and beat it
twice, winning the national championship in their final year, and
concluding with a 27–10 win over Stanford in the Rose Bowl, a
record of ten won, none lost, none tied, against such opposition
as Army, Princeton, Georgia Tech, Wisconsin, Nebraska, Northwestern, and Carnegie Tech.

The Four Horsemen passed on. Notre Dame continued to win.
Others, too, could play the Rockne brand of football and react
to that irresistible fascination. It was not until after 1931, when
this great coach died, that his accomplishment became apparent
in the university's won-and-lost column. Rockne's over-all record
as Notre Dame coach, starting in 1918 and continuing through
1930, was: 105 won, 12 lost, and 5 tied. He fielded five undefeated and untied teams. Two decades later another Irish coach,
Frank Leahy, ran up a string of thirty-nine consecutive victories.
But that was later—much later. It was Rockne who broke the
ground and taught his boys the best and brainiest football that
had been seen up to his day, and then fired them up to play it
beyond anything that had ever been experienced before.

How was this accomplished?

It was again the combination of the times, the psychological
climate, but above all the man. For over and beyond the personality of Rockne, pumped up by the publicity flacks of Notre
Dame, and believe me there was some pumping, there was a
genuinely unique individual. In the games played by Notre
Dame under Rockne, and in particular those classics against
Army, there were some brand-new elements introduced: humor,
affection, and a curious kind of sports love that manifested itself
in odd ways.

Notre Dame played hard, rough, out-to-win football, but many
of their players were witty and great kidders and often put their
opponents out of stride with their sallies. The team spirit of these
boys was tremendous. They sacrificed and blocked for one another, fought for one another, but in a strange way they loved
their enemies too, and could be chivalrous because their coach
was a chivalrous man.

Earlier, when Army was playing Notre Dame at West Point,

Rockne's version of the shift was throwing the soldiers badly off balance, instigating complaints that it was an illegal maneuver.

It was not actually so, for Rockne never played illegal football, but after the first half Referee Tom Thorpe said to Rockne, "I just don't know what to do about that shift of yours, Rock. The Army is on my neck that it's illegal. I know it isn't, but it's so close that it's difficult for anyone but an official to judge."

Rockne said, "All right, Tom, I'll tell you what we'll do. We'll play the second half without the shift."

They did and scored the same number of touchdowns as in the first half.

This was the kind of story which appealed so strongly to the people we were then.

Rockne was a very moral man and we were just emerging from a period when morality was still adjudged a virtue. An ebullient substitute scored a touchdown, and as he raced across the goal line, he raised five fingers to his nose and cocked a snook at the pursuit. Rockne yanked him and took his suit away.

He was moral in the sexual sense, another characteristic of an era which once denied entrance to a European countess on the grounds of "moral turpitude" because she'd had a boy friend. He closed down a *maison de joie* known as "Sally's," above a feed store on La Salle Street in South Bend, as having a deteriorating effect on the neighborhood. The police dragged their feet when requested to cooperate, since apparently some kind of profit-sharing plan was in operation. When repeated appeals failed, Rockne made another suggestion. Either Sally's closed, or he would bring his football team down and take the place apart. The threat of this kind of publicity shook the city fathers to the soles of their shoes, and Madam Sally's establishment took over premises in another town.

Rockne was known for his psychological warfare and the sentimentality of his dressing room pep talks, two of the most famous of which are revealing. In one, after his team had taken a first-half shellacking and sat waiting for the blast, Rockne merely poked his head in the door of the dressing room and remarked quietly, "Oh, excuse me, ladies! I thought this was the Notre Dame team." He was a master at reducing swelled heads,

UNDERWOOD & UNDERWOOD

. . . and suffered when things went wrong—first half of the game with Northwestern, November 22, 1930. Final score: Notre Dame 14, Northwestern 0.

and when his Four Horsemen had an off day, he would suggest that they carry their press clippings onto the field with them and read them aloud to the enemy.

Another famous dressing room oration concerned the plea from the dead—"Go out and win this one for the Gipper, boys!"

According to the legend, George Gipp, probably the most celebrated football player ever developed at Notre Dame and coached by Rockne, lay on his deathbed from pneumonia brought on by overindulgence in all manner of things, and dying, is supposed to have said to Rockne, "If you ever need to win one badly, ask the team to go out and do it for me," etc. etc. The whole thing sounds apocryphal, but quite classical for our times and the kind of treacle we loved to swallow. Actually, the real deathbed story was quite different. Rockne, holding the boy's hand, said, "It must be tough to go, George," to which Gipp replied unequivocally, "What's tough about it?"

At any rate, it was currently acknowledged that Rockne had

Rockne's most famous backfield—the Four Horsemen of Notre Dame: Miller, Stuhldreher, Crowley, and Layden.

used the "Win this one for Gipp" plea and the boys had come through.

What was not common currency was that George Gipp, in addition to being a brilliant football player, was a very bad little boy. He was everything that a Notre Dame college boy ought not to be, a womanizer, a pool shark, a card player, a gambler, and a drunk, and Rockne was attached to him. And with this love for a sinner who could deliver the goods on the football field, any phonyness in Rockne's morality falls away and he stands exposed to us as a genuine human being.

How the great Gipp regarded these dressing room orations

was told to me privately by a contemporary of those days when, in 1920, Rockne found himself ten points behind Indiana at the half, after an undefeated season in 1919.

The coach went into his locker room oration and was in full swing when he noticed that Gipp was not anywhere around. He finally located him standing in a doorway, leaning against the sill, looking bored as he flicked cigarette ashes outside.

Rock was speechless but the Gipper said, "Aw, these pep talks are O.K., Rock, I guess, but I got two hundred bucks bet on this game and if you think I'm lying down out there, you're crazy!"

It was one of the few times when Knute Rockne was struck dumb. In the second half Gipper went out, scored two touchdowns, and drop-kicked the points. His two hundred dollars were safe.

But the story of how Gipp was able to place a wager, an act which today would have gotten him disqualified not only from amateur but from professional football as well, is even better. He had "agents" who did his betting for him, and they reported that for the Indiana game at Bloomington, the gamblers wanted no part of Notre Dame or brother Gipp. The "agents" were planted in the local betting emporium where, the night before the game, a tall, muffled figure with his overcoat collar turned up, marched in and shakingly demanded a Bromo Seltzer, in those days a popular cure-all for hangover. He shivered, and with trembling fingers raised the glass to his lips, swallowed, coughed, gagged, and finally after downing it, staggered out of the door. Someone asked, "Who the hell was that wreck?"

Here, an "agent" volunteered the reply, "Why, don't you know? That's George Gipp. He's been like that just about all week. I doubt if he'll get into the game at all tomorrow. It won't even be a contest without him."

The whole thing, of course, was an act. Gipp hadn't had a drop, got his bet down, and collected the money.

The Gipper could make a living out of pool room hustling and did. He bet heavy sums of money on the games in which he played and spent more time carousing in off-limit South Bend hangouts and saloons, and card-playing, and eventually he was expelled from Notre Dame. But upon Rockne's plea and the passing of a stiff oral examination, he was readmitted.

The friendship between the nineteenth-century-type tough-guy Americano and the soft-spoken, twentieth-century Rockne was the stuff of which our stories were made.

Rockne had the ability to associate names and faces and remembered hundreds upon hundreds of boys. One of his old students recalls the day when nearly six hundred boys went out for freshman football. Rockne divided them into eleven sections, in accordance with the positions they said they played. When these formed groups, Rock asked each one his name. The following day, when they assembled, Rockne had them form a huge circle, and without notes called out every one of them by name and assigned him to the proper assistant coach.

Five days a week between twelve-thirty and one o'clock in the afternoon, in the basement of the old library building, Rockne conducted skull practice in a football clinic. He and Hunk Anderson would pose hypothetical problems of rules and situations and ask for solutions, and it was through these sessions that Notre Dame players acquired such a knowledge of every aspect of the game that they were able to take advantage of any situation which might develop on the field.

Small boys hanging about Cartier Field got into the second half free, until the empty seats were filled. But there were some who passionately wanted to see the first half as well. In those days members of the team ran from the locker rooms onto the field swathed in blankets, and it was not unusual to spot two big cleated feet under one of those coverings surrounded by four, or six, smaller feet, trying to keep in step. Rockne would never see this. Some of these stowaways later became Notre Dame stars themselves.

He was a brilliant raconteur and was in tremendous demand at Rotary luncheons, Lions Club dinners, or any large stag function where men got together to feed and listen to after-dinner speeches.

Added to all of this was the fact that the public at large believed him to be something of a wizard, for there certainly seemed to be magic connected with his successes. Everything he touched turned to gold. He wove his spell over his own players and produced strange miracles, such as the time Tom Walsh, his All-America center, once played the entire last half of a game with two broken hands. But what were crippled digits compared to love of Rockne and the determination not to let him down?

FPG

Knute Rockne with the President Emeritus of the Notre Dame Subway Alumni and Rooting Bund, Mayor James J. Walker.

Not a single bad pass was charged against him through this whole agonizing half.

Knute's influence extended not only to his own squad, but during his all-too-short career as a coach, many hundreds of thousands of other young men warmed their own competitive spirits at the bright fire of this man who stood for everything that was right, good, and successful in American sports of his era.

All this, of course, led to the cult of Rockne. Just as the melting pot of Assistant Noter Damers and hoi polloi alumni attached themselves to the Notre Dame team, so Rockne became their Shaman and High Priest, and was worshiped, back-slapped, and adulated wherever he went. The phenomenon was unique. Much of the fame of Notre Dame of today rests upon his shoulders, because of what he did and was.

And withal, just like with the other great champions who populate this volume, even though you collected and enumerated their extraordinary qualities, skills, and abilities, there was still that mysterious intangible that made them into these special people.

The record of Frank Leahy in the decade 1940 through 1949 was hardly less than that of Rockne. But there was no Leahy cult that I can remember. He was simply a popular, successful coach of a famous university. It was Rock the pioneer who had that extra-added, super champion quality which was unforgettable. I can see him still today, with his squashed-in nose (from baseball, incidentally), jug-handle ears, and humorous mouth, striding the Notre Dame sidelines during a game, or deep in conversation with his second-in-command on strategy as the pattern of victory, or the threat of defeat, began to emerge upon the gridiron. His presence made itself felt. Eleven young men on the field running, kicking, passing, and carrying the ball, but behind them was Rockne.

For all that, the man was no paragon or goody-goody, nor was he faultless. He made mistakes but he never lacked the courage to face up to them and admit his errors. He could apologize to the world or to the most humble freshman candidate. But his faults fade into insignificance today beside the memories of his towering character and ability.

At forty-three his life came to an end, far too young, when on a flight to the Coast from Kansas City, his plane crashed into the Flint Hills in a fog. Perhaps a character so unique and adulated was fortunate to quit the scene at his peak. Certainly his passing marked the end of that particular football era with its newborn excitement. It is all different now. The great school at

South Bend is continuing to score successes. What it does or doesn't do is still newspaper copy. But that vital spark, the electric force and the personality that was Rockne is no longer there, and somehow not even the Subway Alumni and all of the Assistant Noter Damers seem to care quite so much any more.

Queen Helen.

CHAPTER **8**

Helen Wills

Considering that when the thirteen colonies seceded from the British Empire to form the republic of the United States of America, divorcing themselves thereby from royalty, titles, and all the folderol connected with this ancient establishment, the words "king" and "queen" have remained as much a part of the American language and concept as they have in those countries where such still exist.

Having turned our backs once and for all upon any but elected officials, we thereafter, at least in the times of which I write, took every opportunity to identify ourselves as much as possible with what we had scorned. The number of proletarian kings and queens that blossomed in our newspapers was amazing. Any commercial tycoon who achieved prominence was immediately anointed and thereafter referred to as the "Rubber King," the "Automobile King," the "Frankfurter King." And any doll whose measurements approximated 36-24-35, and whose face was considered not likely to stop a clock, could get herself nominated "Queen" either by winning a beauty contest or connecting herself with citrus fruits, Florida real estate, soft drinks, cigarettes, or being elected to head the daisy chain on Graduation Day.

There were Mardi Gras Queens, Carnival Queens, Dress Queens, Queens of society, etc., and Movie Queens. This last category was spread so thin that any little fluff who had ever appeared before the camera, if only for an instant, was immediately included in this noble company.

Eventually, of course, this aping of royalty was extended to

UNDERWOOD & UNDERWOOD

Little Miss Poker Face.

*She could also smile and enjoy herself
like a little girl . . .*

*. . . and set up her oppo-
nents for the kill.*

sports and games, as the players thereof became the most famous people in the country. An archaeologist delving into rubble and finding a surviving newspaper headline referring to the King of Swat, or even more alliteratively the Sultan of Swat, might well imagine this a reference to the ruler of some obscure territory bordering on the Himalayas, and would be exceedingly surprised, not to mention put out, to find that the reference was to Babe Ruth, who, of course, was likewise known as the "Home Run King."

This same scientist, probing at the same level of our ancient civilization, would have come across equally baffling allusions to an American female sovereign, namesake of the lovely ruler of Troy, only to establish the fact that back in the 1920s we, the democratic people of the American republic, took a rather simple middle-class little girl, the daughter of a Los Angeles doctor and a socially aspiring mother, and made her a queen. Queen Helen.

Her name was Helen Wills. She was a tennis player and a world champion. Her crown was a white eyeshade worn against the sun on the tennis courts and which became a symbol, a trademark, and a national fad. She ruled over the tennis courts of the United States and England as well for many years, and over the hearts of millions of Americans who had never held a racquet in their hands, or seen a big-time tennis match. She had other nicknames as well, such as "Little Miss Poker Face" and "Our Helen." But it was "Queen" which better fitted the headlines, and Queen she was and remained. It was only when we tried to turn her into an American Joan of Arc as well, when she went abroad to play the reigning French champion, Suzanne Lenglen, that we and she came something of a cropper.

Since we had been a republic for some 180 years, our idea of actual royalty had to be drawn largely from literature and photographs, and it has seemed to me that our physical concept of queens was considerably influenced by illustrated editions of Hans Christian Andersen.

Helen Wills, at the peak of her career, filled the bill to perfection. She was regally beautiful, insuperably efficient, calm, cold, ruthless, implacable, dignified, aloof, strong, ambitious, imperious, successful, and seemed always to be on the verge of crying with the Red Queen in "Alice"—"Off with their heads!" "they" being anyone who happened to get in her way on or off the tennis courts.

Her record was fabulous and is worth glancing over if only for bulk. She won the Wimbledon singles, conceded to be the world's championship, eight times between 1927 and 1938, along with sharing in three doubles titles from 1924 to 1930. She took seven U.S. singles titles in the years spanning 1923 to 1931, and shared in four doubles crowns from 1922 to 1928. She played in ten Wightman Cup matches against British teams, and won eighteen singles against two losses. And to this record must be added French singles championships and a number of small fry tournaments warming up for the big international competitions.

But the above, of course, is just a fraction of the story of who and what she was, and what she meant to many of us.

During this period there were involved enough characters, conflict, and climaxes to fill one of those big double novels, but the high point of it all was unquestionably her meeting with the French champion, Suzanne Lenglen, at Cannes on the Riviera, Tuesday, February 16, 1926. Before it was over it had the rapt attention of an entire nation focused upon it and took on the aspect of a crusade, not to mention yet another manifestation of the eternal struggle between black and white, good and evil, Heaven and Hell.

To understand it better, one must hark back to that time which saw the rise of the girl athlete from practically anonymity to world prominence.

If you will consult the newspaper files of the 1890s or early 1900s, you will look in vain for tales connected with the prowess of women athletes in any field. In agate type you might find the names of winners of golf or tennis matches, a swimming meet, or a running race, an able *equestrienne* at a horse show, but nothing more.

In the first place it was not considered ladylike, or even healthful, for a girl to don a track suit, leap over hurdles, or launch a javelin, and even less so to appear sweaty with her clothes in disarray on a tennis court. But over and above this nobody cared. It was a man's world and women didn't even have the vote. Then the feminists took over, emergence from prudery freed games-playing girls from the burden of hampering clothing, and when the great upsurge in sports took place they were ready to assume their position alongside the men champions, but one that was somewhat different and extra-special, because they were women. We were suddenly as interested, and in some cases even more so, in what made them tick as in our male champions.

This advent of the girl or woman athlete into fame brought a new dimension into the world of sport and sport drama which became a part of the great decade, which if for nothing else, will be notable as the first in which women were equally publicized and honored along with the men. That dimension was one of the basic differences between men and women.

Whereas the French merely cry, *"vive la difference,"* we were concerned with the mental, spiritual, and above all, psychological differences as well as the physical. The last was concerned with the actual anatomical construction of the female and the fact that when it came to running or jumping, or playing violent games, she was the weaker vessel and invariably the male champion in anything could defeat the women's champion. The exception who confirmed this rule and the only woman athlete I ever knew who was as good and often better than the male, was Miss Joyce Weathered, the British Women's Golf Champion.

It was, however, the psychological dissimilarity which made for the most exciting copy and thrilling melodrama.

If one may timorously offer a theory guaranteed to enrage the feminists, the demands and exigencies of nature have made woman a huntress who competes strenuously and unhampered by any rules for available males. Since this same mystery which, for want of a better name we call nature, appears to be interested mainly in the perpetuation of the species, woman as the perpetuating vessel competes fiercely on this level. Some of this atavism she has carried over with her into the world of competitive sports. Man has learned how to lose gracefully; woman less so.

Not that the male enjoys taking a public licking in a game but he has, down through the centuries, evolved a code of sportsmanship (at one period of civilization it was known as chivalry), and feels himself far more bound to its observance than woman. Females never evolved any code whatsoever in dealing with their sexual or husband-acquiring problems, and came into the man's sports world to find themselves not at all adaptable to the codes he had developed. In fact, from time to time many of them found themselves entirely unable psychologically to accede to these. The "id" of their femininity was far too strong to enable them to knuckle under with a smile.

I have seen male athletes throw tantrums, defeated runners weep, football players whose misdeeds had resulted in the loss of the game throw themselves hysterically upon the turf, kicking and clawing, but always after the event and never during. When threatened with certain defeat, the boys would play out the string. The girls not always. A prize fighter who found himself outclassed and absorbing a beating might opt to take up residence on the canvas for ten seconds rather than face further punishment. But at least a blow, or the semblance of one would have sent him there and he would accept the humiliation of a knockout. But he would never turn his back upon his opponent in midround and offer his resignation while on his feet.

Football players continued with broken bones or torn ligaments; baseball heroes were often a mass of tape concealing their injuries beneath their uniforms, and even tennis players who took painful tumbles in trying for a "get," resulting in sprains or strains, would try to hide the hurt and finish the match.

But from time to time competitors on the distaff side would be tempted to quit under fire, rather than give a hated and despised opponent the satisfaction of an untainted victory. And it was a part of this difference that from time to time women who reached the peak of any game actually did hate and despise their rivals.

Two prize fighters who, for fifteen rounds, had been pummeling one another to within an inch of insensibility or often even to the danger of their lives, could arm-in-arm it in nightclub drinking bouts when it was all over. Football teams that had been brutalizing one another for several hours on a Saturday afternoon, including occasional attempts at serious crippling of opponents, fraternized happily after the final whistle. Champions in every sport at least respected their nearest competitors and often formed a genuine liking for them. The girls were inclined to be less chummy.

All this leads up not only to the splendid animosity that featured the one and only meeting between Miss Wills and Mlle. Lenglen, but the violence of the emotions of love and hatred lavished upon the two partisans by a large proportion of the citizens of the United States.

You would have a difficult time today in making a villain of the woman who was Suzanne Lenglen, even though she had some unattractive qualities, such as arrogance, a tendency to pick her spots, and a further inclination to quit when the going got rough. Actually she was more to be pitied than scorned, as the old song went, for she was the victim of a father who tyrannized her into becoming the world's greatest tennis player with unending practice sessions and scoldings. But for the rest, she was the kind of Frenchwoman that Americans admire today, even though they are usually terrified of them. She was chic, cultured, intelligent, witty, and uninhibited. She smoked cigarettes, liked to dance, drink wine and cognac socially, and was not above a nip at the flask at the umpire's chair between sets, when she felt her spirits or muscles flagging. Unfortunately, she had no looks whatsoever, a hatchet face and a hook nose being her lot, but like all Frenchwomen she dressed so divinely that her ugliness became almost an asset.

But remember the times, our puritan heritage, and what was being turned out by the film studios in the vicinity of Sunset and Vine. The movie vamp was a figure known to us all. She wore slinky clothes, her eyes were made up to look like Cleopatra's in her palmiest days, her mouth as though it had absorbed a bucketful of paint. Her cigarette was always inserted in a long jade holder. She spent most of her time draped over a chaise longue, and when she kissed, the censors reached for their shears like cowpokes for their six-shooters. She was always the cause of some poor slob's downfall and became as familiar a figure to the American public as the country ingenue in apron and poke bonnet, or the simpering expression and long, innocent curls of Mary Pickford.

Helped along by the sportswriters, the appetites and the ingenuousness of our readers, this Frenchwoman of the petty bourgeois class, one who if it came to looks couldn't have vamped a sailor marooned on a desert island for twenty years, was ballyhooed into a bitch composed of Pola Negri, Theda Bara, and the Medici gang all rolled into one, added to which and most reprehensible of all, she was one of them thar, frog- and snail-eating furriners.

And into her exact opposite, the easily recognizable, ingenue heroine we made that Helen Wills who came out of the West in 1922.

She was originally a leggy, breathless girl prodigy with her hair in brown, ribbon-tied braids down her back, who grew up to win the U.S. singles championship in 1923–24–25, and in 1926 went on the stalk for the only woman player said to be better than herself. She neither drank nor smoked, nor kept late hours. She didn't douse herself with perfume, buy her dresses from Coco Chanel, or have her hair frizzed in beauty salons. She was a 100 per cent clean, soap-and-water, virginal American girl, and the night before her match with Mlle. Lenglen prayers for her victory ascended from the hearts of millions of fellow countrymen.

Living as I do today in a world so changed and looking back upon who and what I was, and what I believed during those times, I find it hard to credit this mass outpouring of love and hatred that centered around these two women. And yet it was so, and the files of the newspapers of that age will bear me out. Today we are not able even to transfer our fear and hatred of communism, indicative of a truly titantic world clash which is affecting all of us, to the realm of sports. We compete with the Russ in the Olympics and in great dual track meets. We find the Russian athlete a pretty good fellow by and large, even though we tend to consider him something of a professional and ourselves the white knights of amateurism. But the fact is that we really don't care very deeply. It is more a matter of chauvinism than emotional involvement. But oh, how we cared about the outcome of the trial of strength on a tennis court between Wills and Lenglen.

A face of classic beauty.

With that longing we had then for ten-twent-thirt melodrama, we succeeded in turning what should have been no more than the finals of a completely unimportant French winter resort tournament into a combination of *Ben Hur*, *Lucia di Lammermoor*, and Fireman Save My Child.

Press associations from the Côte d'Azur hinted of wicked plots afoot, intrigues, nerve war against Our Helen; gambling interests, professionalism, sinister characters surrounding the naughty, flighty Frenchwoman. Added to this were accusations that the U.S. tennis authorities were failing to back the brave girl and had abandoned her so that she stood alone against the sharks of the Riviera. Boadicea in her heyday never had a press like Helen Wills. It helped to establish her as the biggest U.S. tennis box office attraction on the distaff side.

Recently I have come to know Cannes very well, since I live on the Côte d'Azur, and while it has changed considerably in the last forty years, Our Helen certainly stepped into an atmosphere unlike any she had ever encountered around and about tennis in the U.S.A. The outside gambling interests were probably exaggerated, though of course there was a casino, but the *ambience* of Cannes in those days was rakish to say the least, and sexy to suggest the most, even as it is today. While the bikini had not yet been invented—and we had just emerged from the shock of the "Annette Kellerman"—the place had not yet been taken over by American film moguls and their wives or popsies. It was far gayer, more highly perfumed, and a greater stronghold of high society certainly than it is today, when society there and elsewhere can only be described as low.

It was the perfect setting and breath of life to a Frenchwoman like Suzanne Lenglen: parties, galas, intrigues—mostly of the boudoir kind—gorgeous clothes, money to burn. Suzanne was at home here. Helen Wills was not.

We felt this back in the United States, indeed it was written and the feeling was of a white lamb in the midst of ravening wolves.

Thumbing back through the sports columns I wrote some thirty-nine years ago before this match, I find my pen dipped into the sheerest heliotrope hysteria. My bill for purple ink must have been appalling. Interest in the outcome of the duel built up beyond anything I have ever experienced, before or since, and one felt that if Helen lost, flags should be half-masted, places of amusement closed, and a period of national mourning instituted.

Alas, she did lose. Suzanne beat her 6–3, 8–6, in a thriller which reversed the fictional happy ending. In the second set, Miss Wills had her opponent on the hook and let her get off. Several times, it was reported with righteous horror, when Mlle. Lenglen changed courts, she paused by the umpire's stand for a little nip of *eau de vie,* to stimulate her flagging endurance.

Had Helen Wills won, she would have been awarded a welcome home against which even those bestowed upon Lindbergh and Gertrude Ederle would have seemed pallid. But the best example of how puffed up with ballyhoo the whole business was, was the fact that the nation survived the loss and actually did not seem greatly to take it to heart. "Our Helen" then went on to become "Queen Helen," the unbeatable; Mlle. Lenglen to fade, burned out, her frail strength overtaxed by too much tennis, to die at the age of forty of pernicious anemia.

The two women never met on the courts again. But Helen Wills established a record of eight wins at Wimbledon which has never been matched. And she inaugurated a series of battles with another Helen, Miss Helen Hull Jacobs, initiating one of the deadliest and most dramatic, continuing, feminine feuds ever to engage the undivided attention of a nation that reveled not only in sport, but the personal stories of those who indulged in it.

One of the truly unique coincidences of the Golden Decade was that it produced not only champions of superior caliber, but at the same time threw up challengers who were of almost equal skill and tenacity, providing situation drama which kept us on the edges of our seats for ten uninterruptedly thrilling years. The one short, sharp clash between Helen Wills and Suzanne Lenglen was an explosive, heart-stopping theater. The continuing struggle between this same Miss Wills and her persistent runner-up, Helen Jacobs, was a long-running suspense serial, the like of which no magazine was able to supply.

And this is why this particular era had to be dubbed "Golden," for the protracted fight, the spiritual as well as the tennis battle between these two girls, sent floods of dollars and pounds coursing through the box offices of the amateur tennis clubs of both Great Britain and the United States.

What kind of person was this girl of close to half a century ago, who made such a remarkable impact upon her country and her times? I promise you she was one of the most astonishing creatures ever to froth to the top of our great American melting pot.

As a young girl in her formative years she was thrown in with a set of really dreadful people. For if ever you wished to find yourself surrounded by a crowd of arrogant, self-satisfied, nose-in-the-air stuffed shirts, windbags, and narcissists, you had only to hang about the marquee at Forest Hills during tournament time. They all tried to talk like stage Englishmen, wore exquisite clothes, and were mostly either rich or the equally fancily decked-out scroungers who hang about the wealthy, aping their manners and hoping that some of the money will rub off on them. They looked down upon the press as a necessary evil, barely acknowledged the tennis writers from the *Times* and the *Tribune,* and all but spat upon us lads from the tabloid *News, Mirror,* and *Graphic.*

Such an atmosphere could hardly fail to have an effect upon a young girl who, had she not been compelled to endure the publicity due to her skill at tennis, might have grown up into a normally agreeable young person, distinguished for perhaps no more than her extraordinary beauty.

Bill Tilden loathed her. Two men, Fred Moody and Aiden Roark, loved and married her. She could be gay and sunny, yet the face she showed an admiring public was cold and implacable, her expression of studied non-expression unchanging in victory or defeat to the point where the press nicknamed her "Little Miss Poker Face."

When she had an opponent going she was as ruthless and relentless a killer as was ever Jack Dempsey, and never for a moment revealed mercy or pity. She went to the top and stayed there, not only because she could hit the ball hard and accurately, but because every girl who faced her across the net was not merely a match opponent, but someone in the way of Helen Wills.

She had the reputation as well as appearance of being completely glacial, unemotional, and implacable, and yet, I in the company of a few other sportswriters once saw an almost incredible Helen Wills with her hair down.

The situation arose out of a friendly, tea time, clubhouse argument as to how good was a good girl against a good man. There had previously been a kind of practice match between Miss Wills and a tenth-ranked man player by the name of Fritz Mercur, played under the agreement that Mr. Mercur would keep away from the net. Helen beat him and Fritz thereafter took an unmerciful ribbing. All this took place during the course of one of the national championships at the West Side Tennis Club in Forest Hills.

Word got around somehow that Miss Wills was going to give Mercur a chance to regain his lost manhood by playing him a return match, no holds barred. In other words he was to be allowed to go up to the net for cut-off volleys, smashers, and placements. Some of us got wind that this extracurricular affair was to take place on the center court an hour or so before regular play began, and we were there early to see the fun.

Mercur won, which was not surprising, but to our utter astonishment the cold, hard, unemotional girl romped like a kitten, trying to match the agile Mercur at the net and shouting with laughter at her losing efforts. It was the one and only time I ever saw Helen Wills having fun playing a game of tennis.

Her manners toward the press, I thought, left considerable to be desired, but so did those of most of that Forest Hills crowd in those days. And her glacial coldness toward her opponents may have been no more than an indication of her supreme concentration on the game and winning. Yet it may have been that very self-concentration that enabled her to remain at the top as long as she chose to do so.

She had the courage of a lioness, the stoicism of an Indian brave, and the beauty of a Greek goddess. It was this beauty which at one time attracted me and led me to squire her upon several occasions when she decided in the mid-1930s that she had sacrificed sufficiently upon the altar of the West Side Tennis Club with its assorted stuffed shirts and jackanapes, and wished to live it up a little.

I invited her out just so that I might sit beside her and drink in the lovely, classic line of her profile, and we toured one or two traps in New York, such as The Stork Club and El Morocco. However, even during that short-lived rebellion, her alcoholic indulgence was limited to nursing a thimbleful of green crème de menthe through an entire evening.

I remember one night, when we had been dancing together at El Morocco for what seemed to me like two solid hours non-stop, since bands infiltrated one another for continuous playing. My legs were aching, my wind failing, my tongue hanging out, but I wasn't going to quit if it killed me, for it seemed at last I was managing to make an impression upon Miss Wills, at least as a prancer if not as a Young Man of Manhattan. At this point she looked me coolly in the eye and said—"You know, Paul, this is awfully good for my footwork," reducing me to the level of a sparring partner who was not only keeping her in training, but through avoiding being squashed by my big feet, aiding her to perfect those mincing steps she used to flit across court in pursuit of a hard drive.

Big-time tennis in that era had a curious pattern of some of the girls chickening out when the going got rough, or it looked as though they were about to be defeated by someone they considered their social inferior. Suzanne Lenglen had quit cold to Molla Bjursted Mallory when the Norwegian tigress had her licked in the first set and two games love in the second. In 1934, in the finals of the women's national singles championship at Forest Hills, Helen Jacobs, the perpetual runner-up to then Mrs. Helen Wills Moody, had at last achieved one set up and had a big lead in the second when Mrs. Moody, complaining of an injured spine, defaulted set, match, and championship and walked off the court. Miss Jacobs was denied the satisfaction of, for the first time, beating her old rival and in straight sets at that.

With a whoop and a holler, we, the columnists and gentlemen of the press, descended upon Helen Wills Moody—erstwhile "Our Helen"—and gave her back to California. In the twinkling of an eye so characteristic of the public vs. champion relationship of those days, Miss Jacobs was elevated to the position of national heroine and Mrs. Moody consigned to the role of the villainess of the play.

It is interesting to look back at events now sifted through the fine mesh of so many years, to note how wrong we were, how moved and swayed less by facts which could have been checked or ascertained, than by the glory of the big headline and the ever-beloved tale of the mighty fallen and the lowly raised.

The mootness of just how severe this spinal agony might have been is, I am afraid, still debatable. For what was never generally known and may not be even to this day, is that Mrs. Moody proposed to continue the following day in the women's doubles, partnered by Miss Elizabeth Ryan, and was only dissuaded from doing so by the good and common sense of this same Miss Ryan, who pointed out that for Helen to quit one day and appear for championship competition, even for the somewhat less strenuous game of doubles, on the following one, would leave her wide open to the most violent and unpleasant type of press criticism. Mrs. Moody had the good sense to scratch.

However, the fact remains that athletic backs are tricky things. They can deliver you into the hands of a thousand devils one day and the next produce nothing more than an occasional twinge and sometimes not even that. One particular twist or motion during the continuation of the match with Miss Jacobs might have aggravated the condition to the point where if applied, would have resulted in unbearable pain. But by the next day it could have as completely calmed down and might have given the girl no difficulty whatsoever during a doubles match. The press, however, would have given her plenty of trouble.

Mrs. Moody's error lay in ever entering the championship that year, or in not defaulting to Miss Jacobs before the match. The truth was that she had injured her back some time before. After the event she went into a hospital in California for an operation, and spent three months in a plaster cast and a year away from tennis. She quit because, with good reason, she was afraid of permanent injury. But even morally she was entitled to do so. For if you will insist upon the amateur letter of the law, you have no right to complain if at any point in a tournament a player lays down his or her racquet, says—"I'm not having fun any more"— and departs.

Mrs. Moody not only wasn't having fun, but she was in pain.

On the stalk. Mrs. Moody leaves for Wimbledon.

The fact that a sellout crowd had paid large sums of money for admission to see her play was, strictly speaking, none of *her* business. She was not under contract playing for a fee. It might indeed have been the business (though it never has been) of the bodies charging the entrance money, to print upon the tickets: "These players are amateurs. No guarantee of their appearance can be furnished nor of their completion of the tournament."

And so, for the wrong reasons at the wrong time and at the wrong place, Mrs. Moody was pilloried, whereas at many another time she might have been taken to task and was not, for her rudeness to Miss Jacobs or her lack of interest in the game except where it concerned her own career.

But coward? Or quitter? Not she. I remember that winter I paid her a visit in San Francisco and she drove me about for an afternoon in her car, proudly showing me the beauties of her city. Never once did she complain about the beating she had taken from the newspapers, or by word spoken or unspoken intimated that she had been hurt. She never at any time revealed resentment or replied to the insinuations that she had robbed Helen Jacobs of her victory through sheer feminine malice.

But in the spring of 1935, Mrs. Moody quietly packed her tennis kit and set off for Wimbledon. No one could say that she was on the prowl for Helen Hull Jacobs, for Wimbledon is always a tourney of upsets and there was no guarantee that she and Miss Jacobs would meet in the finals. But a stalk it was, nevertheless— to the kill. *That* kind of courage and indomitable will power you must love and respect.

Certainly, in those days we never had to invent or puff up the great sports dramas. They simply seemed to happen, one after the other, in every kind of game or contest. Believe it or not, and had a novelist or dramatist devised it he would have been told off for corn, the two old rivals who so detested one another actually did meet in that Wimbledon final. They won a set each and Miss Jacobs was leading 5–2 in the final one, with 40–30 advantage for match point.

Off a forcing shot by Miss Jacobs, Mrs. Moody barely reached the ball to raise a sitter that floated over the net for her opponent to kill, for game, set, match, and all the marbles in the Fem-

Her two greatest rivals—
Suzanne Lenglen—
and Helen Jacobs.

inine Fury Stakes. Mrs. Moody stood there and stared defeat in the face and the end of the long, patient comeback trail. She was a dead pigeon. There were no nerves, no weak backs, no defaults in the midst of that losing final set however, but just a girl who could take it waiting for her rival, whom she disliked, to put the ball away.

And then the overeager Helen Jacobs played the shot known to every week-end tennis dub. She smashed the ball into the net. It was all the old lioness needed. Mrs. Moody pulled out the game, won the next four to take the Wimbledon title, 6–3, 3–6, 7–5, and with that gallant, wordless gesture replied to every criticism that had been leveled at her on the score of her default the year before. *That* day she was truly a queen.

And yet . . . and yet . . . One sad, final coda to the look backward at this strange, brilliant, courageous yet inexplicable woman, as reported by the late Bill Tilden in his biography, *My Story*. On that fateful day in 1934 when Mrs. Moody defaulted, Helen Jacobs, meeting her at the umpire's stand, ". . . put her hand on her shoulder and said,—'Won't you rest a minute, Helen?'

"Miss Wills coldly replied, 'Take your hand off my shoulder,' picked up her racquets and left the court."

"Finest people you ever seed, come to the Garden patronizing old Tex."

CHAPTER **9**

Tex Rickard

(1871–1929)

This is an estimate of the Tex Rickard I knew in the long ago, the onetime cowpoke, gold-rusher, Alaskan sourdough, and gambling saloon proprietor who became the world's most fabulous boxing promoter.

In his dramatic and glamorous lifetime he elevated the sport from the stench of the Horton and Frawley Law era of wretched smoke-filled dives to a glittering, royal extravaganza perfumed by the smell of the rich.

With Jack Dempsey as his bellwether, he staged the biggest spectacles, produced the greatest dramas, and racked up the most awe-inspiring scores for attendance and gate receipts in the history of boxing. However, in the story of those times and the part Rickard played in them, he must share the limelight with that arithmetical concept and onetime goal of every American— a million dollars.

America has known several boom-and-bust periods in the twentieth century, but the postwar one which began in 1920 was the first genuine inflationary joy ride to affect a society that was going through many startling changes, and altering its face practically before our eyes. With a dirty war in which we had not been too badly hurt safely behind us, we were ready for a whale of a time. A more lax morality or, shall we say, the first tolerance of immorality, took a great leap forward at that period and so did the human passion for gambling. The stock market was one enormous roulette wheel and everybody was betting red or black, bulls or bears, including my office boy, who handled the race results on the *News,* and used to telephone his broker regularly every afternoon.

Money, which heretofore had been sluggish, hard to come by, and the subject of lugubrious lectures on thrift with the general theme of a penny saved was a penny earned, suddenly became free, loose, and fluid. Everyone could make it, or lay his hands on it, and having acquired some, teach it to multiply. Finance took on an entirely new aspect, from something restricted to somber blokes in top hats known as financiers, to a game that anybody could play. For the first time it seemed that the Midas touch had become universal.

A million dollars today is considered change out of a billion, to be dropped into the petty cash box, but following World War I and the thrilling, magical, market rise, it was the be-all and end-all of our existence. "Million dollars!"; "millionaire"; "shoot the million" were the most beautiful words in the English language. The backers of the new Madison Square Garden in New York were known only as the "Six Hundred Millionaires," and in writing of the crowd that hung about boxing, Westbrook Pegler put together the satirical combination of "Rich Million-aires." These were the barons, earls, and dukes of the American postwar aristocracy.

It was a new kind of gold rush, other than the one in which Rickard as a young man had participated in the Far West and during the opening up of Alaska. Money, like the unicellular organism the amoeba, was splitting, reproducing, and doubling itself overnight on the exchange boards. We were emerging from a time when one hundred thousand dollars was considered the competency. Now the magic figure of a million was the goal, with its marvelous properties of self-perpetuation—no more worries. Coupon-clipping for exercise; money piling up in the bank every time the clock ticked.

But this was the gambler's approach to "get rich quick." In his early days, Tex Rickard had run gambling houses for the gold miners of Alaska and Nevada and had already learned all there was to know about the money fever that infects men.

He knew that next to women, nothing is as stimulating or interesting as money, and he used its sparkle as bait. This, too, was a hangover of the rough, tough, sourdough days when all that glittered was indeed gold; when the cartwheel silver dollar was

. . . and the reasons why.

the medium of exchange, and the miner, fresh from the field, threw his poke of dust or nuggets onto the table.

The modern gambler, curiously, doesn't want you to think that it is cash with which you are playing and hastily translates it into chips, or plaques, to promote the concept of a harmless game. It is something to see in the foreign casinos how quickly a yellow hundred-franc note dropped onto a number is whisked from the table by the croupier and replaced by that impersonal chip. Rickard used the thrill of large sums, even though the era of specie was over and money had become only bits of paper. But each of his shows had the aura of gold about it, and the huge guarantees he offered his performers, the price of the tickets, and the magnitude of it all produced a feeling of excitement that made his productions practically irresistible.

Million dollars, million dollars, million dollars was like the tolling of a great bell through all of them. And the hysteria reached its ineffable climax when he paid that sum to one prize fighter for thirty minutes of exercise and 104,943 persons shelled out $2,658,660 to see him earn it. Overnight, from September 22, to September 23, 1927, Gene Tunney, who had been a nobody, became a millionaire before the eyes of the world, as it were.

At the time all this happened I was a part of it, so to speak, certainly a part of Rickard's ballyhoo. The hundreds of sports columns I wrote about his promotions as well as reports of his fights, certainly contributed to the buildup at the box office, as did those of all of the other sportswriters of our time. Hence I was far too close to the situation to see what is so eminently obvious today. One can almost put it in the form of a syllogism: poor people are unimportant; rich ones are important; if poor people get to be rich people they become important. Tex Rickard took the poor prize fighter and made him into a rich prize fighter, whereupon the pugilist automatically became a person of prominence.

Today we are used to this phenomenon. In the higher echelons of the ring there are no poverty-stricken pugs. Prior to the 1920s they were practically all ham-and-eggers, knocking one another's brains out for comparatively small purses. They were champions perhaps, but in the minds of the general public, small fry mugs and bums about whom it was not worth bothering one's head. Nobody gave a damn about them and never, unless they managed to stop a bullet or run amuck with a carving knife, did any of them manage the long journey from the sports section to page one.

They were the concern only of Sports, bartenders, and small boys who wished they could be like John L. Sullivan, Bob Fitzsimmons, or Jim Jeffries, when persecuted by bullies. They impinged not one wit upon the middle classes and certainly never came within a country mile of setting foot upon the threshold of Society, with a capital S. By the simple gesture of making his fighters wealthy, Tex Rickard altered all this and thereby guaranteed himself an interest in their doings, both in and out of the ring. By handing them these vast sums he initiated a kind of perpetual-motion ballyhoo and buildup which was working for him night and day, even when he had no great ring extravaganza in prospect.

In what I have now grown used to calling "my day," everybody knew who Andrew Carnegie was, John D. Rockefeller, and J. Pierpont Morgan, not to mention the Vanderbilts, the Du Ponts, the Whitneys, et al. They were millionaires. But only a minute percentage of the populace could have identified Ad Wolgast, Jack Dillion, Jimmy Clabby, George Dixon, Freddy Welsh, or Johnny Coulon.

John L. Sullivan, onetime heavyweight champion, with his "I can lick any man in the house!" impressed himself somewhat upon the national consciousness, but subsequent heavyweight bruisers until the advent of Rickard did not. They fought for small crowds and purses. Jack Johnson managed to acquire quite a file in newspaper morgues because of scandalous conduct and brushes with the law, but no one gave a button otherwise for the private lives of champion pugilists in any of the divisions. They were inconsequential people. Rickard dusted them with gold, and thereafter the glitter never left them.

From that time on it became as impossible to ignore a fighter laying his championship on the line as it was to disregard a big Wall Street proxy battle which might result in the change of control over million-dollar properties. For the latter was an exact analogy of what was about to happen when two of Tex Rickard's highly paid performers stepped into the ring. Control over a million-dollar asset, the title itself, was at stake and was liable to change hands at any moment and with considerable violence. As many in the crowd were drawn by the financial implications as by that violence.

It was something to have been there when fighter X dropped his left just a shade too low after a lead, giving fighter Y the chance to cross his right, and ten seconds later fighter X, after his head cleared, could be contemplating a loss of from three-quarters to two million dollars in futures. By making his hirelings big businessmen themselves, Rickard packed his fifty-dollar ring-side seats with tycoons of trade and commerce, come to watch their like transact their little deals in public.

Not all the colorful champions and fighters who performed for Rickard became millionaires, but they did earn huge purses compared with the peanuts that were collected before his day, the little men as well as the big. They now wore fine clothes, owned their own homes, drove about in expensive cars, and also took on added importance from that high point of the era when Gene Tunney earned one million dollars cash for providing his end of an evening's entertainment.

Whether or not Tex knew what he was doing, or it was instinctive, the point is it worked and accounts in great part for the tremendous success of his promotions. You might not be interested in boxing as a sport or spectacle, but it was no longer possible to ignore the men who engaged in it. They were now wealthy and hence people of standing.

For this was, after all, the ultimate dream of our times—the fast buck. Tunney's million was, and still is, the fastest buck in history. Actually the famous check that Rickard handed Tunney for services rendered was for $990,445, some paltry $9555 short of the round amount. But the champion's cut of radio and movies and other by-products brought his fee well over the seven figures.

George Lewis Rickard was born on January 2, 1871, near Leavenworth, Kansas, but his family moved to the Texas Panhandle and by the time he was ten years old, he was almost on his own. He became a cowpuncher, acquired his nickname, worked his way to independence as a cattleman, and threw it all over to join the Klondike gold rush.

It was still the old West then; rough, tough, and lead-slinging, and Rickard had what it took to survive. But instead of digging for gold, he gambled for it and ran what were called Emporiums of Chance in Dawson City, Nome, and later Goldfield in Nevada. There was gold, gold, gold everywhere. Rickard handled that yellow metal in eagles, double eagles, nuggets and dust from the miner's pokes. He saw it ebb and flow and its effect upon humans.

If you will study the rise of successful men from poverty to wealth, you will become aware of a pattern of affinity between certain individuals and money. They can be broke a half dozen times, or in debt, or even jailed for one or two losing bouts with some of the trickier laws that govern finance, yet in the end they are always back again with another million or two, building up a new fortune. They seem to exercise a mesmerizing power over the flow of currency and have an enormous ability to divert it their way. Rickard was one of these and I should say one of the more astonishing ones, since he dealt in no really tangible commodity that provided a basis of any security in speculation— something needed by humans such as food, medicine, clothing, housing, oil, or real estate. Tex had nothing to offer but at most a forty-five-minute period during which time there might be one or two thrills, with no guarantee whatsoever of same being included in the price of entry. There was no protection against a fifty-dollar ticket being an admission to an hour of boredom, or even fraud. And yet he sold them by the thousands.

On September 3, 1908, Rickard staged his first fight for the world's lightweight championship between Joe Gans and Battling Nelson. The citizens of Goldfield, Nevada, having acquired a sudden thirst for notoriety, wanted to put their town on the map and came to Tex for help. He knew that boxing got a lot of publicity and suggested the idea of the Gans-Nelson bout to be held there and then. With that inspiration of the born *entrepreneur*, he dumped the full amount of the purse to be split between the men, thirty-two thousand dollars, in ten- and twenty-dollar gold pieces, into the window of his saloon. Goldfield was on the map and Rickard had found his profession and the confessed ambition, sometime in the future, to produce spectacles that would rival in grandeur the ancient Greek and Roman games.

Rickard never forgot the compulsion exercised by large sums of cash, or the lure of the yellow metal. Twenty years later, he remembered to emboss the backs of his tickets for his outdoor fights with gold. They were large, heavy, imposing-looking, and felt like money.

There were two phases to Rickard's career of fight promotion: the western, beginning with the Gans-Nelson fight, then Jeffries-Johnson at Reno, Nevada, and Willard-Dempsey in Toledo, and his attempts to break into New York, which he succeeded in

The gambler turned promoter in San Francisco. Rickard in center. At his left is James J. Jeffries, who became heavyweight champion of the world.

The early Rickard. A theatrical group in Alaska. Tex is second from the right in the front row.

doing in 1920 when he acquired the old Madison Square Garden, and boxing in New York State became relegalized through the passage of the Walker Law. This was the beginning of the fabulous decade.

You may visit Madison Square today, in the vicinity of Twenty-sixth Street and the East Side, but you will find no trace of that wonderful edifice known as "old" Madison Square Garden, because of the construction of the "new," which still stands at Forty-ninth and Fiftieth streets and Eighth Avenue.

An office building has been reared in its place. But it was a romantic pile with a high bell tower, within which the architect, Stanford White, was shot by Harry K. Thaw as punishment, I believe, for monkeying with Madam Thaw, giving rise to one of the great *causes célèbres* of the early 1900s. It served as an arena as well as an exhibition hall. Here I saw my first circus, that of Messrs. Barnum and Bailey, and also my first prize fight and strangely, one which ended in tragedy and death, just as the first baseball game I ever saw likewise ended in the death of a player, Ray Chapman, as the result of a bean-ball thrown by Carl Mays.

The boxers were two featherweights, Buddy Taylor and Frankie Jerome, and if I close my eyes I can still see black-haired Jerome, helpless but clinging to the ropes with one hand so that he would not go down, and the blond Taylor belting him unmercifully until at last Jerome lost consciousness. He never thereafter recovered it.

And fight night at the old Garden brings up memories of the elephants. For once the circus had occupied it in the spring, they never did get the odor of the big pachyderms out of the building and it was there for keeps, just as it was the scent of horses at the old Pioneer A.C., another boxing *boîte* on the East Side, not far from the Garden and which had originally been a horse market and auctioning hall.

Physically, Rickard was a most engaging person, a tall man with small, twinkling eyes set into the bland, smooth-skinned Texan's face. He had the gambler's thin-lipped trap mouth and usually an infectious, boyish smile and impish expression. His trademarks were a soft, light-colored fedora hat, the snap brim turned down, a straight, gold-headed Malacca cane, and a cigar. I can hardly ever remember seeing him without these three. He kept his hat on indoors and out. And thus I remember him best, standing in the lobby of Madison Square Garden on his Friday fight nights, watching the crowd pour in, his little eyes sparkling with delight as he would say, "Just look at all them wonderful people patronizing old Tex. Finest people I ever seed, coming in here and patronizing me."

He was a born politician and a compromiser. He paid political blackmail when he had to, in order to obtain a license, or a contract, or a stadium. He was not dishonest, but had a business-man's simple, easygoing approach to ethics.

Somehow the city politicians of today don't seem as dread-fully venal and wicked as those of forty or fifty years ago or, if they are, they dress better and know how to manipulate the pinky at a dinner party. But then they were ruffians whose chief occupation was browbeating the immigrant vote and loading ballot boxes. They had their own kind of Mafia. Yet against these assorted gangs, as well as rival promoters, ward heelers, and plain Eastern chauvinists who resented this ex-faro dealer invading their territory, Rickard played a lone hand and won.

There may be many ways of analyzing Rickard's sky-rocketing success, but certain unusual elements of it are not to be ignored. He had a wonderful name: Tex Rickard! It smacks of the wide-open spaces, saddles and cayuses, six-guns and saloons, rustlers, sheriffs, dance halls, and all of that fascinating conglomeration of claptrap that made up the ever-endearing fairy tale of the Far West.

He was a part of that West and what was more, he looked like it and talked like it, even though he dressed as a gentleman. About him was the aura of the Texas range and the still-life of the double-barreled Derringer laid upon the green baize of the card table. He was the dramatic stranger from far-off, exciting places, and the kind of man in whom one wanted to believe. Once again I am compelled to say that along with all the others we have dubbed The Golden People, he had it; that star quality, that difference that makes a man stand out ten feet tall in a crowd, inspires trust and admiration, wins him friends and followers, and enables him to swing the big deal.

Often it is someone's private neurosis, fetish, or feeling of inferiority which ordinarily might emerge only on the psychiatrist's couch which can by accident spark off or contribute the key to some mysterious success. Deep down Tex Rickard was a social snob and a social climber. It was not in the sense of caring to break into the ranks of society as Tunney did, but just as he said, wanting to be patronized by them. It made him feel good, who had never had educational advantages, to see the cream of New York's strata come to him to buy tickets for his shows.

Tex was a keen businessman as well, who knew how to equate business risks with gambler's odds. Prior to this time only tennis and polo had touched the pockets of the wealthy. Rickard was determined to get at some of the gold in them thar folds. Besides which, it was in the air. This was the period when it was either

Damon Runyon, or one of his characters, who advised one to
hang about exclusively with rich people, on the theory that some
of it might eventually rub off.

Rickard made his play for the rich by promoting a charity
match for Miss Anne Morgan, a sister of old J.P., who was raising
funds as head of the American Committee for Devastated
France. He pitted Benny Leonard against Richie Mitchell for
the lightweight title, proceeds to go to war-stricken France, and
for the first time the nobs packed the old Garden and were
treated to one of the most thrilling brawls in lightweight title
history. Next, he signed fair, handsome, war hero Frenchman
Georges Carpentier to fight dark, beetle-browed, shipyard worker,
villain Dempsey. And finally, in his most brilliant professional
gambit, having led women to want to attend his prize fights, he
made it possible for them to do so.

We, in this sheltered, sanitary age, have simply no conception
of the atmosphere of turn-of-the-century prize fighting; the low
dives where they took place, the stink of unwashed bodies and
the dangers of toughs and knuckle-duster wielders, pickpockets,
drunks, cokies, etc., who frequented them. It was worth your
life to go; you never got the seat your ticket called for and, of
course, the places were filthy.

I never saw any of the old Horton and Frawley Law holes,
where boxing was conducted around the turn of the century, but
some of the smaller clubs I used to have to cover at the beginning
of my tenure as sports editor of the *News* were places where you
wouldn't want to take no ladies, such as the Coney Island A.C.,
the Star Casino just on the edge of Harlem, the Pioneer A.C.,
or even the St. Nicholas Arena, which also doubled as an ice-
skating rink.

When it came to roughneck joints the Pioneer was my favorite,
for it was a long, barn-like hall which, as noted before, served
double duty as an auction room and horse market for everything
from delivery wagon crocks to the big Percherons that still
hauled the drays, trucks, and brewery wagons in those days.
There were two narrow balconies which overhung the ring so
closely that one could almost lean down and touch the fighters.
The place was so small, smoke-filled, smelly, and intimate that

it was really like watching a couple of boys having it out in the barn, back of the house. Occasionally one might spy a woman in the crowd during fight night at the Pioneer, but you could bet that she would be big, buxom, brassy, and blonde.

These were the joints where the club fighters battered one another silly for sixty or a hundred dollars and where the main-eventers would only qualify as preliminary contestants at Rickard's Madison Square Garden. But they fed the Garden, and a lad who made a reputation in any of these clubs could soon work himself up onto the Garden card and become a headline attraction.

Exciting though the brawls held there indeed were, the audience was practically restricted to men, like George Bellows' famous painting of "Stag Night at Coney Island." This was the vestige of what low-class boxing was like just before Rickard came to New York.

Tex changed all this. He hired a chief usher by the name of Willie Stillman, who rehearsed his large, uniformed staff for months. His tickets bore portal, aisle, section, and seat number. In charge of his box office he put a quiet, moon-faced young man named Joe Boyton, hired away from the Ringling Brothers' Circus. Special police and guards were on hand for protection and to keep order. It became as safe for a woman and her escort to attend a Rickard fight as it was to go to the theater. Two tickets were now being sold where only one had been bought before. The foundations for the first million-dollar gate had been laid.

As he had discovered in his youth in Nevada, when he had displayed what then was a vast purse in gold, bigness made for more bigness and thus he parleyed huge sums into overwhelming crowds. When he guaranteed Dempsey and Carpentier the up-to-then unheard-of sum of half a million dollars for their participation in a ten-round fight in New Jersey, everyone thought he was crazy, even his backers, who withdrew. Yet the mere fact that this much money had been put up led so many people to go to see this crazy man fall on his face, as well as to witness two pugilists who could earn that kind of cash in thirty minutes or less of quarreling, that they produced the up-to-that-time largest crowd and gate in the history of boxing—eighty thousand souls and receipts of $1,789,238. The million-dollar gate was a reality.

By the process of its own giantism, in the same manner as money in millions multiplied itself, so the large crowds drew larger ones and became almost in themselves an attraction. That still unbroken record draw of 120,757 people crouched in the rain and the darkness behind the ring lights of Philadelphia, where Tunney relieved Dempsey of his title, made for a spectacle and a tale to tell, and to have been a part of it was to have been touched by the excitement and fascination of the times. When next Rickard invoked the partnership of Dempsey and Tunney at Soldier Field in Chicago, he drew $2,658,660 in paid admissions. This was high-water.

My mind carries me back to those incredible, wacky days in Chicago at the time of this promotion and Rickard's suite, occupying an entire floor of the Blackstone Hotel. The corridors and rooms were filled with ticket-seekers; rich and poor, carriage trade and bums, politicos, gangsters, tarts, managers, fighters, gamblers, flesh peddlers, with Tex and his gold cane, hat, and cigar visible only occasionally, blandly beaming. For the rest of the time he conducted his business with the key figures of the promotion from the lid of the john in one of the bathrooms—the only place where he could achieve total privacy.

There was another self-perpetuating element to help Rickard to these extraordinary records, and that was the free publicity he garnered through the columns of the press. He had a curiously innocent and childlike attitude toward newspapers. He felt that he was entitled to publicity puffs and praise and was deeply hurt when any of us suggested that a card scheduled for one of his Garden *soirées* or, for that matter, a projected heavyweight championship fight, might turn out to be a stinker. He would say, plaintively, in his soft, Texas drawl, "You fellows oughtn' to be knocking. You ought to be boosting my shows. What you fellows always around knocking for? Knocking don't help no one."

Whatever, the truth was that by mid-decade he had us all

on the hook with his Midas touch, the expanding universe of
his productions and the exciting, dramatic stories connected
with everything to do with them. If we had not reported and
commented upon them, we would have lost readers right and
left. If the free space he thus profited by had been calculated

*The world's greatest boxing promoter in his office at Madison Square
Garden the year before his death.*

in terms of paid advertising, there would have been yet more
millions at which to marvel.

Certainly the times were ripe for this kind of extravagance.
If Rickard, Dempsey, and company had happened along after

the financial collapse of 1929, or say the whole association had been postponed for ten years, a sobered-up American might have declined to shell out from twenty-five to fifty dollars for so-called ringside. Since that time prices have been even more exaggerated, to seats of $100, and one reads that the top for the recent Liston-Clay fight was $250 or $500 for a pair, which might indicate that anyone indulging could be considered a case for commitment. Inflation, however, has drained the color and the glamour from the million-dollar gate. The champions of today appear to contribute little to restore it and even if they did, somehow we cannot seem to care as deeply any more.

Tex Rickard died on January 6, 1929, leaving behind him as a monument a new Madison Square Garden, the super sports arena of the age, now already considered obsolete and about to be replaced. It was another one of Rickard's dreams realized, with its modern gadgets, icemaking machinery, and terrazzo floor, which Tex so loved. When it was being put in he came every day, like a child with a new toy, watching over it and patting it.

There was a scandal in Rickard's career, during his early days as a promoter in New York, which needs no raking up here except as a measure of his personality and how far he had come from his beginnings as a cowpuncher and gambler. He got himself into a mess with some rather nasty little teenage chippies in what could have been either a frame or blackmail attempt. The point is that some of the best people in New York appeared upon the stand to testify to Rickard's character, and in the end the jury brought in a verdict of acquittal.

The man whose life was one long, uninterrupted drama expired unspectacularly in Miami of a gangrenous appendix. He was brought up to New York to lie in state for twenty-four hours in the center of the arena he had built, his painted mummy looking not at all like him, on view to the public. To me the oddest of all the phenomena connected with him were the thousands who shuffled endlessly past his bier. I could never quite determine whether they came because Rickard's last show was free, because they were curious, or because they had a genuine affection for this stranger from the West. Whichever, they were the rear guard of a vanished era, and the late Rickard one of the chief representatives thereof. The crash of 1929 had been only a few minutes away, so to speak, and thereafter the good days got old very quickly.

Tyrus Raymond Cobb, the Georgia Peach.

CHAPTER **10**

Ty Cobb

(1886–1961)

Not to start an argument, but in my opinion, looking backward, Tyrus Raymond Cobb, whose sports nickname was "The Georgia Peach," was the greatest baseball player who ever lived.

One may come forward with one who has a better record in this phase of the game, or more of a stylist in that, but added to the fabulous collection of cold, statistical figures Cobb amassed in his lifetime there was the man himself, a unique and compelling character who infused such life, flesh, and blood into the chill digits that his like has not been seen since.

Actually in his career he bridged two decades, but he both played and was manager into the nineteen twenties, to join that group of extraordinary champions who in accomplishment, glamour, and fortune are looked upon today as The Golden People. Ty Cobb was the first (and so far as I know only) millionaire ballplayer.

The fact that he made his money through intelligent investment is neither here nor there. What so startled and tickled us was that we were living in times where a ballplayer *could* become a millionaire.

And now, with hindsight and many further revelations about this astonishing man, what is even more startling to contemplate is the likelihood that during that time we were observing what might have been a somewhat mentally deranged athlete.

It was recognized that he indulged in some very odd conduct off the field, such as carrying a gun and engaging in constant quarrels with his family, friends, and employers, as the Detroit

sportswriters of that era knew and mostly refrained from printing. But it is, perhaps, the most perfect commentary upon both
our times and customs that none of us became aware, solely from
watching Cobb's baseball play and what we knew of his feuds
and fusses, that the traumatic experience of the shocking death
of his father, coupled with the brutal hazing he, young Cobb,
received at the hands of his fellow players when first he joined
the Detroit Tigers at the age of eighteen, could have left him
neurotic or, as they might have put it in Georgia, "tetched in the
haid." The point being that against the background of that decade and the sports personalities thrown up by it, Cobb did not
appear to be at all strange.

And if you ask me how such neuroses manifested themselves,
I can only say by his very perfection on the diamond, coupled
with the truculence and savagery he exhibited to attain it. Baseball has never been a gentle game indulged in by gentlemen,
and there are moments of hard body contact and others of danger where serious injury is possible. To *that* side of the pastime
Cobb brought a fury, cruelty, and a viciousness heretofore un-
encountered even in the roughest kind of play. True, he used
this frenzy as a part of psychological warfare, aimed at shatter-
ing the nerves of his opponents. But there was nothing synthetic
about this. There was a burning rage in Ty Cobb never far from
the surface, and it flared redly in competition. His compulsion
to excel was far beyond anything which had been seen perhaps
in any sport, and therefore might fairly be considered a wide
departure from the average.

To begin with, at the risk of being told off from all quarters,
I would venture a statement that no great sports champion is
wholly normal. A 100 per cent concern with a game to the ex-
clusion of all else is surely tinged with obsession. The single-
mindedness necessary to fight one's way to the top, in no matter
what sport, is something not shared by the majority of mortals.
And then there is the exhibitionism.

All of the champions developed during those days were looked
upon as very special people. Men like Babe Ruth, Bill Tilden,
Dempsey, Tunney, even girls like Helen Wills, Gertrude Ederle,
and Babe Didrikson were distinctive characters and so far dif-

The young Cobb and friend, before the roughnecks of baseball had put the steel into him. The friend later became President of the United States, Cobb its batting champion.

The famous Cobb batting grip.

*Lightning on the
base paths.*

ferent from the ordinary that, as we have seen, we made kings and queens of them. We had, for instance, a middleweight champion of the world by the name of Harry Greb, who was really a most peculiar kind of fellow and led a very unorthodox life both in and out of the ring. And as for baseball, it certainly had its fair share of screwballs, like Rube Waddell and Babe Herman, to mention only two. The very fact that all of our great champions were "different" was what helped to make them such interesting and exciting people to us.

Thus, when viewed against such a background, the curious behavior of Cobb toward his fellow players, his owners, the press, everyone and everything connected with baseball and his extraordinary competitive fire, did not seem too peculiar. And whatever may have been the state of his mental health and his emotional leakages, the fact remains that in every way, physically and technically as well as intellectually, he was the most efficient, competent, and consistently sensational ballplayer of all time; greater even, I suspect, than Honus Wagner, who was the performer to whom Cobb looked up.

His impact upon baseball, his fans, and his times were both immediate—in each and every game in which he appeared *something* dramatic and exciting happened—as well as accumulative. Through some twenty-four years of outfield play Cobb piled record upon record, and by the time he intruded upon the second decade of the twentieth century, he was practically a museum piece of legend and achievement. You have only to glance over his lifetime averages to be aware of the enormous treasury of games played; at bats, hits, runs scored, runs batted in, and bases stolen stored up in this one man. And even then you, today, will have no inkling of the games he won, influenced, or inspired by sheer force of personality that swayed not only his own teammates but the enemy, luring them into errors and misjudgments.

If Babe Ruth was the best-loved player of all time, Ty Cobb was the most hated, and in our story-book era must go down as the undisputed champion of the heavies. The boos that he caused to ascend from partisan haters in the stands must still be ringing through outer space.

He was the most aggressive, tryingest, never-give-up, get-the-hell-out-of-my-way fighter who ever rattled a pitcher, stole a base, or tore into home plate, spikes high. There isn't anyone even remotely like him operating on any diamond today, or probably even living, for the breed he represents, the old-time, half-ruffian ballplayer, is no more. Nor is the game the same as it was fifty years ago, and unless the fans begin to tire of the long hit, and the rule-makers and ball manufacturers return to the former type of play, we shall never see his like again.

In every other sport, practically, the old records have been wiped off the books and performers have appeared who have outdone the athletes of the twenties by the stopwatch. But before there can be another Cobb, the home run must be de-emphasized both via the properties and content of the baseball itself, as well as the construction of the parks. It would be easy enough to deaden the ball, but no one is going to tear down modern stadia to eliminate the high-fly, windblown home run which, in the old days, would have been an easy putout.

As we have seen, what made Ruth's early achievements so sensational was that he was hitting the old ball out of the lot, not the beefed-up, jack-rabbit article later altered to suit the demands of the fans for the novelty of the long ball and the quick breakup of a tight game. No one knows exactly when the missile was changed, but it was sometime during the mid-twenties, when home run hitters suddenly popped up throughout both leagues.

But Cobb was also hitting much more difficult pitches than are permitted by the rules today. Ball doctoring, such as the use of saliva, or slippery elm, the emery ball, the shine ball, the licorice ball, or the one with its horsehide scratched by fingernails or torn against spikes to make the pitch dipsy doodle just before the plate, are forbidden today. The throw comes over dry and its flight foreseeable, if the pitch has been diagnosed correctly as to what kind of spin has been imparted.

Perhaps the most succinct and possibly oversimplified way to sum up the difference between baseball today and that of fifty years ago, is to say that ultramodern strategy is to put men on base ahead of the heavy hitter, so as to bring about a multiplication of runs when the big one goes booming into the stands.

Runs are sought for in clusters. Half a century ago the strategy was all directed toward putting a man onto second base, once, by whatever means, hit or walk, he had reached first.

It was not the batter so much who was important, as the man who had gotten on ahead of him, and players, coaches, and managers concentrated on the task of moving him around until he crossed home plate. This was accomplished by a kind of internal baseball; the steal, the sacrifice bunt, the hit-and-run, the double steal, and the squeeze play. Anything went to get a man across, including the pressure of terror. Every stolen base set up another potential score.

But, in today's game, if the man at bat is a long-ball clouter, why risk a putout as the result of a steal gone wrong, or waste an out with the sacrifice? Neither players nor managers are conditioned to think in terms of a one-run win and to work for that run. In Cobb's time it was his skill upon the base paths and the fear he inspired which made him such a star at that kind of game.

Cobb on first and leading off for his headlong plunge for second, could and did throw the opposition team into such a state of jitters that its effect was felt long after he had made his famous hook slide, one spiked foot high, to safety at the next bag. There was no telling into how many errors or wrong decisions the defending team was forced later on by the shakiness engendered by Cobb's attacks.

Fans are always trying to compare Babe Ruth and Ty Cobb. This is absurd since they are incomparable, say like trying to draw a resemblance between an elephant and a wolf. You might hold, if you liked, that Ruth was a better elephant than Cobb was a wolf, or vice versa, but that is about as far as you may get. They played differently and with far different objectives. Each constituted a distinct and separate threat to the opposing team, the Babe with his physical bulk, timing, and extraordinary batting eye that could break up a game with one blow and win it with the uncatchable ball; Cobb with his strategic edge and terrifying behavior on the base paths, which made not only the enemy pitcher, but the team jittery and so angry that they worked off balance.

Even now that he has passed on and half a century has rolled by since the days of his prime, it is difficult to assess Cobb's true character, except to be certain that he *was* a character and a mass of paradoxes. Perhaps the animal comparison above ought to be turned about and Ty should be thought of as the elephant and, if so, he was the rogue of the herd.

Besides my own memory of him, this estimate leans heavily upon his singularly interesting biography, *My Life in Baseball: The True Record,* written with Al Stump and published in 1961, and a brilliant article by Stump in *True* magazine of December 1961—"Ty Cobb's Wild Ten-Month Fight to Live." Many of the modern generation reading this today would probably recognize Cobb as highly neurotic. But forty or fifty years ago psychiatry was in its infancy, psychology a word confined to the university campus, and when we encountered such a one as The Georgia Peach who fought with everyone—teammates, opposing ball-players, his bosses, newspapermen, umpires, and spectators, we merely wrote him off as a cantankerous so-and-so and a fellow to keep away from, rather than someone who was ill in the mental sense and unadjusted to his environment. To us who were contemporary with him, it seemed that Cobb was simply more of one than others.

And, actually, in those days how much of a this-and-that Cobb was and the right or the wrong of his actions depended a good deal upon what town you were from, and in which ball yard you happened to be sitting. To a Detroiter, Ty wore a halo. It was the visitors from St. Louis, Boston, Washington, New York, and other American league towns who appeared horned, tailed, and cloven-hoofed. To the Detroit fan, when a rival player lay on the ground weltering in blood from a ten-inch gash in his thigh, inflicted by Cobb's spikes, it was—One of theirs and not one of ours, and why didn't the dope get out of the way? To adherents of the injured one, Cobb was a murderer.

Cobb's own defense of himself in his book, his actions, style of play, and the brannigans in which he was involved, are a glimpse into the depths of a strange human being. From it emerges a sad and bitter history of a boy who once had ideals, manners, and gentle upbringing and who had them broken on the wheel of the stupidity, brutality, and jealousy that was rife in baseball and its players at the turn of the century.

Tyrus Raymond Cobb came from an old Southern family which traced its initial immigration to the New World back to the beginning of the seventeenth century. He idolized his father, William Herschel Cobb, who was a schoolmaster and mathematics instructor, respectively, in the towns of Lavonia, Harmony Grove, Carnesville, and Royston, Georgia.

Ty always referred to his father as Professor Cobb. It is not known where schoolmaster Cobb earned his professorship, a title much misused in the United States, particularly in an era where vendors of patent medicines as well as orchestra leaders were known as "the Professor." But he was an educated man, a scholar, an aphorist, and something of a Bible-whacker, and from all descriptions a stern, honorable, and upright man. The father-son relationship here was not unusual at the century's turn. Father was Jehovah. Young Ty both loved and feared him and at all times most desperately desired his respect and praise.

The young Georgian knew that he had disappointed his parent when he drifted, at a very early age, into playing professional baseball in the minor leagues down South; bitterly disappointed a man who had wished him to attend first a university in Georgia and then enter the Military Academy at West Point. But Cobb Senior was of the stuff that could swallow his frustration and counsel his son that if indeed baseball was to be his life's work, then he must make good at this, never dishonor his name, and strive to be the best.

Unquestionably it was this advice and his father's kindness in unbending to a young boy in a career crisis that triggered off the Ty Cobb that was to be.

For the early Ty of the minor leagues—Anniston, Augusta, etc., was a clean-living, gentlemanly, soft-spoken lad who was polite, listened to his elders, kept out of brawls, and lived by a series of precepts given him by his parent.

He liked to quote his aphorisms: "Never commit an act that might degrade your dignity or belittle your manhood," and "Starve and drive out the evil demon that lurks in all human

What a Cobb slide looked like.   C⟨

blood, ready to rise and reign," or, "Be under the perpetual guidance of the better angel of your nature. Be good."

Cobb was also fond of Polonius' advice to Laertes: "Beware of entrance to a quarrel; but being in, bear't that the opposing may be aware of thee."

He played good, hard, winning baseball, learned his trade, attracted the attention of big-league scouts, and in August of 1905 received the news that under other circumstances would have sent him into an ecstasy of happiness, namely that he had been sold to the Detroit Tigers.

The unique coincidence of five of the leading hitters of their time in Boston for one game. Left to right: Ty Cobb, hitting at .386; John Collins of Boston, .529; Ike Boone of Boston with .370; Joe Harris of Boston, .421; and Harry Heilmann, Cobb's teammate from Detroit, with .452.

The other circumstances consisted of a ghastly family tragedy. For back in Royston, from accounts of the catastrophe, Professor Cobb apparently did a very curious thing for a man of honor, integrity, and nobility. He suspected his wife of infidelity and even more astonishing, he set a horrid trap for her

Announcing that he was going to a neighboring village on business and would spend the night there, he climbed into his buggy and drove away. Instead, he went only a short distance, to await darkness and what might be considered the time of assignation.

But Mrs. Cobb was entertaining no one and according to local testimony never had. His suspicions were completely unfounded. She was asleep alone, when a dark figure appeared at her bedroom window and put a leg over the sill.

Unfortunately, there was one friend in the room with her, the ubiquitous companion of women by themselves in rural districts, where the wandering tramp or degenerate and quondam sneakthief was an ever-present menace—the double-barreled shotgun.

Awakening with a start, terrified by the shape climbing through the window, she reached for the gun, presented it, pulled the trigger, and blew her husband to kingdom come. He died before he ever knew that his son had reached the eminence desired by every ballplayer: the major leagues.

And Cobb himself admitted he had never gotten over his father's death. No modern psychiatrist would ask for more when plumbing for a cause of illness.

But there was yet another reason for the change that came over the formerly quiet and mild-mannered boy. He came into the game at a time when the stars were for the most part ignorant, hard-boiled, hard-drinking, foul-mouthed, brutal, tobacco-spitting toughs, and they offered the young son of a Georgia scholar and educator the choice of becoming like them or being persecuted and hazed out of the league. They were stupid men, and the beatings and indignities they inflicted upon the youth turned him for life into a surly, sour, bitter, and hot-tempered rebel, and brought to the fore a streak of cruelty and violence that was to plague him through all of his life.

Here these two elements, the terrible death of the only man he ever really loved and respected, coupled with the hostility of men who should have been his friends and mentors, combined to produce a ruthlessness, the like of which is not to be seen on any modern diamond, and a white-heat competitive fury which was completely abnormal. Every moment of his playing life he was out to prove himself to his father and confirm the

confidence Professor Cobb had shown in him when he let his son
go his way as a ballplayer and even aided him financially. At the
same time Ty was in a way avenging himself upon his tor-
mentors by a perpetual antagonism toward the world.

This resulted in the most marvelously aggressive player temperament in the history of the game. Every second that he was
in there, he was all out to win, physically, mentally, intellectually, and psychologically. He was 100 per cent dedicated in the
field to making the putout, getting on base when he came to bat,
and thereafter coming home with the run. It is safe to say
that Cobb regarded baseball not as a game, but as some form of
war and total war at that. When he was on the field he just about
abided by the rules of the International Red Cross, so to speak,
but beyond that it was "Katy bar the door." From the moment
the umpire called "Play ball!" until the final "out," he regarded
the nine men of the opposing team as mortal enemies and behaved toward them as such. The failure of partisan fans, visiting
players, umpires, baseball writers, and rival managers to put
themselves into Cobb's frame of mind was *theirs*, not his.

The rules give the runner the right of way on the base paths.
Cobb insisted upon these rights. It was up to the man with the
ball to fathom the direction of his slide, avoid the steel knives
fastened to the soles of his shoes, and tag him out. Ty never
gave quarter, but like his contemporary Dempsey, whom in all-
out, destructive, killer instinct he resembled, he never asked for
it either.

As an attraction, this truculent aggressiveness and unquenchable will to win made him nonpareil, even though the spectators
pretended that they disapproved of his tendencies to undress in-
fielders and catchers with his spikes. For with Ty Cobb on first,
flashing suddenly down the base path for second, or hitting the
dirt for home plate, it was somewhat like being present at an
automobile race; there was always the chance that one would
be witness to an accident.

We claim to be a quiet, peace-loving people, but actually we
love violence. Any time Cobb was playing, in addition to the
thrill of the unorthodox move in which he specialized, there was

always this enticing possibility that someone (including Cobb himself) might get hurt. This would bring forth managers and trainers running onto the field carrying the little black first-aid bag; there would be blood, bandages, players crowding around the victim, cries for vengeance, incipient brannigans or riots, and all of the gorgeous attendant hullabaloo to make up a thoroughly delectable afternoon for the fan.

Cobb was probably the first ballplayer who understood and practiced psychological warfare in the nth degree. His opponents retaliated by trying to make *him* look bad to the public, and succeeded. Ty didn't care how he looked as long as he won. He was not, I repeat, *not* unfair. He was a better sport than most.

His personality, particularly toward the end of his career, was tough, leathery, and repellent, a man with a prickly exterior who suffered fools badly. Looking over some of the old sports columns I wrote back in 1928, I find that in company with Westbrook Pegler, I interviewed Cobb on the field before an important Yankee-Athletics series. He was leaning over a box talking to a friend when we asked whether we could fire a couple of more or less personal questions at him. There was nothing friendly in his face as he said, "Yuh cain if yoh write 'em the way ah answer them."

Then I asked him whether he had a million dollars, the kind of idiocy I used to deplore when perpetrated by others. But the very fact shows our preoccupation with that magic million. Still, those were the days when somehow the acme of a reporter's brilliance was to ask a ballplayer before a World Series, or a boxer on the eve of a championship defense—"How do you feel?" a sure interview killer if there ever was one. Cobb was not pleased and suggested that inquiry into his finances was just a mite too personal, which indeed it was.

He had that million too, stashed away in stocks and bonds, and this also was part of the Cobb who spent the major portion of his lifetime placating that poor ghost wandering about in the hereafter with his head blown off. Not only must he succeed in his chosen profession famewise, but likewise with fortune as well, and he played with money as furiously and intelligently as he did with bat and ball.

Ballplayers in the past, and particularly in Cobb's time, had been notably improvident. Elevated to the major leagues from obscure and penurious backgrounds, they suddenly found themselves with more money than they ever dreamed of, but no knowledge of how to hang on to it, or multiply it. It was easy come, easy go, with them, and no thought to the days when age would rob them of speed and coordination and they would find themselves unmercifully dumped onto baseball's refuse heap. The most intelligent of them might acquire a farm or a garage, a small business or an annuity, but the majority ended up broke and down and out.

Not Cobb! The furies that infested him drove an already shrewd financial brain that could judge the value of money, to invest what he made in the newly organized General Motors and Coca-Cola companies. The post-World War I boom and fabulous stock market rise did the rest toward producing baseball's one and only millionaire. He did not stop there, but in his later years and after he had retired, continued to play and outwit the stock market in the same way he gauged an opposing pitcher, endlessly searching for and finding weaknesses, trends, and outguessing it on what it was going to do. He died worth some twelve millions of dollars, a good deal of which went to the establishment of hospitals and charitable foundations. He was a man of great contradictions.

During his lifetime Ty was charged with every kind of baseball misdeed, from deliberately putting the steel to opponents, to sitting on the bench before the game and sharpening his spikes with a file. At his door was laid the ruining of careers of rival players by injuring them, drinking, brawling, and that greatest of baseball crimes, going up into the stands and beating up a vituperative fan. As might be expected there was a grain of truth in many of these charges, but most of them were greatly exaggerated. By and large he stuck to the advice of Polonius and let the other fellow start the trouble.

The incident when Cobb *did* go into the stands after a spectator, and was suspended by League President Ban Johnson for it, was sparked by the fan calling out obscenities that simply would not be tolerated today without police action to remove the offender. Cobb was impaled upon the dilemma of his father's reminder not to belittle his manhood and reacted accordingly, with justice on his side.

But so highly were these stories of Ty's villainies regarded that at times he had but to step out of the clubhouse onto the field to call forth a perfect storm of boos and jeers, a glorious catharsis for the spectators. There were moments when he had the on-lookers so riled he had to have police protection to and from the park.

He had to be tough to survive in a tough era. In advising on hitting he once wrote: "I used to love to choke up and smash them at Hal Chase, at first base for New York [this was before the days of Gehrig], the kind that cannon off the knees of an infielder and leave him limping for days."

This is not exactly the sentiment of a gentle, forgiving soul. On the other hand, this wasn't tiddlywinks but professional ball for cash. Let brother Chase or anyone else get their knees out of the way, or meet that kind of aggression with courageous and ada-mant repression, speed and skill, and field the hit for an out.

Cobb, after his retirement, had nothing but contempt for the modern ballplayer, not because he thought him less virile or manly, but because he considered him mentally lazy, pampered, and relying upon the long ball and the short fence to get him out of trouble. Ty himself was the most intelligent, analytical, and "busiest" player in the annals of the game. When he wasn't on the field he was thinking and remembering, storing up informa-tion on the strengths and weaknesses of the men he encountered throughout the season. Nothing was too small or unimportant to escape his keen eyes and brilliant mind.

One or two small examples will serve to pinpoint this. A pitcher bluffed a "spitter" on every throw by first holding the ball to his face. How to tell then, when the ball was coming up dipsy doodle wet, or dry and hot? Cobb worried, speculated, and studied. Then one day he caught something that no one else would have seen in a hundred years. The peak of the pitcher's cap moved ever so slightly when the spitter was coming, as he opened his mouth to apply the saliva. And that was the end of

Cobb at the end of his playing days.

that hurler's effectiveness against Cobb and the rest of the De-
troiters.

Another moundsman was detected keeping his elbows close to
his body when he meant to throw to first, and slightly away be-

fore the pitch to the batter. Out came the elbows and off went
Cobb on his way to another stolen base. It was this "reading" of
the actions of his opponents on the field that garnered Cobb his
fabulous collection of steals, rather than any phenomenal speed,
because at 6 feet 1 inch in height and between 180 and 190
pounds he was too big to be really fast. He didn't need to be.
He was clever.

Babe Ruth is known to a generation still living for his magnificent impertinence in pointing to center field in the World Series
against the Cubs in Chicago, with Root pitching, to mark the
spot where he would park the next offering and then knocking
the ball for a home run out past the flagpole planted there.

Ty Cobb once called the steal of all three bases, second, third,
and home, to a catcher who had been riding him. Each time he
shouted "I'm going down" he took off and after a final yell of,
"Look out! Here I come," slid under him with the winning run.
Each to his own specialty. But which was the more miraculous
feat?

A place hitter who "choke"-gripped his bat with hands apart,
Cobb at one time offered to treat the sportswriters who had been
criticizing him to a little demonstration. On that day, against the
St. Louis Browns, he hit three homers, the next game another
two. Two more balls during this extraordinary and record-
breaking bombardment just missed going over the top of the
stands and fell back for ground-rule doubles. He had simply
slipped his left hand down the bat handle, locked it to his right,
and let go. Thereafter he quietly went back to his safe and scientific hitting that had brought him more league batting championships than any other man. He made the point later that
along with his home run record, the Babe had also struck out
1330 times.

For the emotions, warmth of heart, sentiment, and colorful
copy plus performance, there was the one and only Babe Ruth.

But thinking back to that stupendous decade and its sports
champions, I am still filled with that sense of rare satisfaction
yielded by the play of Tyrus Raymond Cobb, his achievements
and his personality. To his efficiency he added grace, elegance,
and artistry, and if he aroused antagonism, he also compelled

admiration as a male and a fighter who never for a single instant on the field settled for less than complete, all-out effort to win. And now in retrospect I find myself prey to the emotion of pity as well (which Cobb would have despised), for the tortured human being that he was, weighed down with the then unsuspected burden of weaknesses, insecurities, and compulsions. What really matters is the record of the man, and if I am to choose my greatest of the great of baseball remembered, then for all of his faults and even, if you will, cruelty and disregard for his fellow players' skins, I must take the surly, snarling, wonderful old Tiger of Detroit.

Johnny Weissmuller, the human fish.

CHAPTER **11**

Johnny Weissmuller

Mulling over a list of the famous champions produced with such prodigality during that amazing decade from 1920–1930, there is almost an embarrassment of riches. One tends to look quickly through the records of modern times to make sure that one is not downgrading the stars of today, or using the adjective "matchless" too frequently and in general behaving like the club bore, buttonholing new members and bending their ears about the good old days.

But the problem as it developed in this book was whom to leave out, so many outstanding men and women were there at the top of their respective sports, so many memorable characters who left ineradicable marks upon the era.

No one, for instance, could come close to Willie Hoppe at the billiards table, outsprint Charlie Paddock, or outlast Paavo Nurmi at distance running. Earl Sande was a name to conjure with among jockeys, a champion among riders, as was Tommy Hitchcock, Jr. on the polo field.

It was the time of Gar Wood the speedboat king, Sonja Henie the skating ballerina, Walter Hagen the professional golfer, Suzanne Lenglen the French tennis star, baseball pilots such as John McGraw, Miller Huggins, and Connie Mack, and prize fight managers of the caliber of Jack Kearns, Leo Flynn, and Jimmy Johnston.

Unquestionably there are performers today who in speed and skill surpass members of our gallery of old-timers. Yet with all due respect, somehow, they do not signalize the fifties or the sixties.

The reasons why are not difficult to understand. For one thing we seem to have neither leisure nor the peace of mind to concern ourselves so deeply with sportsmen and -women. Sports in the United States today are set in a pattern and one that seems to be undergoing very little change. Each game has its devoted followers, but few have drawing cards of such magnetism that they excite millions of people who have never even seen them play.

Further, one needs only to examine what it was that the Golden People had in common with one another. It was their ability not only to excel in, but to dramatize their sport as well, through the extraordinary power of their personalities. Too, ground was being broken, barriers demolished, new fields pioneered, so that almost every week, month, or year something happened on the field, the water course, or in the arena that had never occurred before.

Thus, even today in the face of Don Schollander, the blond eighteen-year-old college boy who won four gold medals during the recent Olympics at Tokyo, when I think of swimming I remember only Johnny Weissmuller. There were others who felt like I do and what is more, made it official when, in 1950, an Associated Press poll of sports broadcasters and coaches named him the outstanding swimmer not only of his decade, but of the first half of the twentieth century. Such an award is not based upon records alone but is the result as well of an exciting personality, coupled with consistent performance. Along with those others of his era he impressed himself indelibly upon the national consciousness.

Johnny Weissmuller, born June 2, 1904 at Windber, Pennsylvania, was the great dramatizer of swimming. When he retired in 1929, he held every world free-style record from 100 yards to the half mile. He swam on two American Olympic teams, won five gold medals, and in each race broke a world's record. Weissmuller held the outdoor titles for the 100 and 400 yards splashes in 1922–23 and 1925–28, and took the half mile as well in 1925 and 1927. From 1921 to 1929, when he turned professional, *he never lost a free-style race,* an accomplishment, according to his coach Bill Bachrach, unequaled or even approached by any other swimmer in the world. Of thirty-eight men's swimming records approved by the A.A.U. in 1922, eleven of them belonged to big Johnny.

And all through those years of top-flight competition and performance, he was being himself—a character, lighthearted, gay, irresponsible, fun-loving, clowning, overflowing with that mysterious substance we sometimes refer to as "star quality," and an overwhelming competitor. He had that super-champion's magic wallet of reserve upon which to draw when he had to pull out that extra effort needed to win.

If you don't remember him as the then fastest human negotiator of H_2O, and you might not, since every one of his records have since been washed off the books, you might as the moving picture star of Tarzan, and later of Jungle Jim, in which he became world famous and forever clinched his right to the elite company of the Golden People.

Swimming has had a curious history. It was an important sport in times of Ancient Greece and Rome and part of military training, but during the Middle Ages in Europe fell into almost complete disuse, due to the widespread belief that outdoor bathing made one vulnerable to the fearful epidemics that so often swept the continent. It is hard to believe, but the prejudice was not overcome until the latter part of the nineteenth century, practically on the threshold of our era.

Speed in the water is only a recent thing. Prior to modern times, the main idea was to keep afloat and move about in imitation of the frog. In 1893, an Englishman, J. Trudgen, exhibited a double over-arm stroke and in 1900, Richard Cavill, an Australian, added the scissors leg-kick to it and produced the crawl, although it was said that Solomon and Hawaiian islanders were using this method for centuries back. However, the point was that drama came to a heretofore colorless sport. For the first time, swimmers were able to produce a bow wave indicative of speed and thrust.

Swimming needed a Weissmuller. Up to his time there had only been a Hawaiian beach boy by the name of Duke Kahanamoku, to earn a modicum of fame and give a fillip of interest to a means of locomotion which, at the turn of the century, was

The boy from the Illinois Athletic Club.

The Olympic champion. Johnny has just set up a new Olympic record for his day of 58⅗ seconds for the 100 meters free style at Amsterdam, 1928.

still handicapped by Victorian pruderies and, as we have seen, sent its practitioners—the women, at least—into the water weighed down with a load of garments sufficient to sink a seal. It seemed as though Johnny had been deliberately invented and carpentered for the sport. The moment of his appearance upon the scene was perfect. For the first time the spectator, who up to then had yawned his way through the swimming meets, saw a human being actually speeding through the water.

Some of these chapters have noted that several of our great champions were not molded in the classic Greek form which we have come to identify with an athlete's body. The same complaint cannot be registered against John Weissmuller. He was magnificent.

He stood 6 feet 3⅓ inches, pool-side, with wide shoulders, flat belly, no hips or buttocks, long, slender, smooth-muscled legs and arms, and was a dark-haired, dark-eyed Adonis as well.

When I suggested that he was invented for the part he was to play, I meant just that, for his body appeared to have been endowed with a curious and special kind of buoyancy. In the 1936 Olympic Games, we all noticed that Jesse Owens, the great Negro sprinter, seemed to run not on, but across the top of the track. No sooner had his spikes touched the dirt when they were out and reaching for the next stride. It was the same with Johnny Weissmuller in the pool. He swam not in, but somehow on top of the water, his back arching out. He was half human, half hydrofoil, and when he got up speed and his body climbed onto its built-in step, eliminating drag, there was nobody who could catch him.

Shortly after he was born, the Weissmullers moved to Chicago, that lusty, stimulating, fast-expanding, untrammeled city which in itself was to grow into a bellwether of the era and provide most of its excitement on a number of fronts, including sports. It produced three of our great all-time champions and characters: Knute Rockne, Red Grange, and now Weissmuller.

For it was there the boy grew up into a lanky, happy-go-lucky kid who spent most of his spare time on the lakefront with other water rats, indulging in skylarking and impromptu races—"Last one out to the raft is an old maid!" No old maid role for the Weissmuller boy.

When he was fifteen years old he caught the eye of Bill Bachrach, swimming coach of the Illinois Athletic Club.

The athletic club, too, belonged to those particular times, or rather was the product of a prior day when a college education, particularly in the big eastern centers, was the privilege of the rich. If a poor boy wanted to compete nationally or internationally in some sport, he would wear the colors of some organization such as the Illinois or Chicago Athletic Clubs, the D.A.C. of Detroit, the Los Angeles Athletic Club, or Winged Foot of the New York A.C.

These were wealthy associations housed in ornate buildings, providing superb athletic facilities, though most of the exercise taken by members often consisted of picking up cards from the

Look at him go!

table and arranging them by suits. But there was no paradox here of penniless boy joining rich club. For all of these organizations thrived on publicity and press cuttings to attract their paying members. Thus, where technically the universities were forbidden to proselyte, there was absolutely nothing to stop the big athletic clubs from doing so, and they went shopping for name and fame in the persons of young, competing athletes who could win meets and national championships wearing the colors of the club. Such boys, whether they had ever attended a university or not, received gratis athletic membership and the best coaching available at the time to non-collegians. Indeed, the athletic clubs employed some of the finest instructors in the world.

Such a one was Bill Bachrach, engaged to build up the swimming team of the Illinois A.C. On the prowl for likely material, he paused one day to watch a batch of youngsters horsing about in Lake Michigan. One slim seal caught his eye. He had all the adolescent puppy's gawkiness and awkwardness, but he was parting water, his legs churning stern-froth like an old-time Mississippi packet.

Bachrach invited the lad to do a couple of turns in the I.A.C. pool and put a stopwatch on him. After he had examined the dial and pushed his eyes back into his head again, he promptly dubbed Weissmuller Athletic Member and thereby acquired the boy who was to become the outstanding swimmer of his times. But memories of the superb performances of the big man and his ineffable "star quality" and champion's aura have not dimmed.

Bachrach kept Weissmuller under wraps for a year, teaching him the intricacies of competitive swimming, the racing start which can frequently pick up a yard at the gun, and the pool turns, the push-offs which are likewise an integral part of every record-breaking swim and must be performed perfectly. Weissmuller ate it up. Master and protégé became as one, and when in August of 1921 Bachrach officially launched him, he won the 50- and 220-yard national championships and thereafter was never headed.

Like all of these people we have seen who were touched in that decade by this magic fire, Weissmuller had courage and competitive spirit to burn. The nightmare of every speed swimmer is swallowing water which, coupled with the physical exertion and tension, usually brings on black-out and loss of the race. It turned to reality for Johnny in the 100 meters finals in the 1928 Olympics at Amsterdam where on the single turn he dipped too low, breathed wrong, and there it was. The field was all even at the time. Johnny felt himself going. But he opened that champion's wallet and pulled out what was needed. He swallowed a lungful, lost two yards, and then began to churn in the wake of the Hungarian Barany. First at the touch, John Weissmuller, U.S.A., time 58⅗ seconds, a new world's record.

Again at an A.A.U. meet in Honolulu, the I.A.C. needed to take the half-mile swim, the last event on the program, to win the competition. None of the other swimmers on the team was capable of winning this. Weissmuller had already been through his own strenuous schedule, swimming in and winning three races as well as his leg of the relay. He hadn't trained for the 880.

Bachrach called over his pupil and gave him the facts of life and then eyeing him asked—"How about it, Johnny?"

Weissmuller replied with the carefree slogan that was his war cry all through his competitive years (until replaced by Tarzan's weird, treetop ululation which rang around the world) "Le's go!" He toed the tank and plunged in. Winner and new national champion in world record time—J. Weissmuller, Illinois Athletic Club.

Swimming never became the spectator sport to draw great crowds that tennis, golf, polo, or track and field did in the wake of the stars, for there were not yet the big water amphitheaters, and essentially a swimming race was slow compared to other means of locomotion. Nevertheless, the fame of Johnny sky-rocketed.

And he was actually a star ahead of his time, which is why many of his marks lasted far longer than those of any previous swimming champion. The reason that swimming records were and are so ephemeral was that forty years ago the techniques of the various strokes were just being developed. Man was learning how to become fish and from fish, advance to torpedo, and it was Weissmuller who raised the whole level of the sport to show what could be done and pave the way for all of the faster men to come.

And come they did indeed, one by one to lower Johnny's records by seconds. For instance, Weissmuller's hundred-meter mark of 57⅘, when last seen, had been reduced to 53.6 by Manuel Dos Santos of Brazil in 1961. But without wishing to offend our big neighbor to the south, who has heard of Senhor

Don Santos since? Johnny's other marks are usurped by a variety of names and nationalities. The point at which Weissmuller joins the company of greats is when it is realized that Johnny held *all* of them at the same time over a ten-year period. It's the old, old story all over again. There are golfers today who make better scores in championships than did Bobby Jones and tennis players who hit the ball harder than Tilden. But where are those who have the day-to-day winning consistency to rank No. 1 in whatever their line may be over a decade?

Weissmuller was one of the best-natured and most untemperamental super-athletes to bask in the limelight of the kind of publicity we turned upon such in those days. He remained unspoiled, and during the years that I knew him I cannot remember him ever being unkind, petulant, or swellheaded.

He never laid claim to being an intellectual or deep thinker and his pleasures were simple, beginning with women, with whom—to borrow a phrase from the late James Branch Cabell—he "dealt fairly." He married some four of them: a Mexican film actress with the disposition of a hot tamale by the name of Lupe Velez, with whom his marital battles made newspaper headlines, Bobbe Arnst, a dancer, Beryl Scott, a society girl, and finally, Allene Gates, a golf champion. He liked fast cars and had a childish preference for the expensive kind of practical joke, like turning in false alarms, for which he once became embroiled with gendarmes in Coral Gables, Florida.

He was also a clown and comic of high order, and had he not caught on as Tarzan, he might have become a funnyman. He and Stubby Kruger, according to L. B. De Handley, former Olympic and Women's Swimming Association coach, broke up the Olympic Games in 1924 in Paris by putting on a comedy swimming act plumb in the middle of the races. The crowd went wild and made them encore it twice, while officials turned purple at the disruption of their schedule. After that it was barred. That year Johnny had nothing more important on his mind than winning gold medals in the 100 meters free-style, 400 meters free-style, and 800 meters relay, hanging up a world record in each. He never failed to be there, properly unclad, when the starter raised his gun. When not involved in such appointments, however, he was sometimes difficult to locate, since the field for getting up to mischief in Paris was practically unlimited.

He was able to dub his own Tarzan films when they did the German version, for his family background was Austrian and he could speak perfect German, but what is not generally known is that he also performed all his Tarzan stunts himself. Those powerful gibbon's shoulders were just as useful in swinging from tree to tree as beating up an Olympic pool. He wasn't put off by anything, no matter how dangerous, and once vaulted onto the back of Mary, a three-thousand-pound, ill-tempered M.G.M. rhinoceros, and rode her for a scene, after she had injured two of her trainers previously and chased four others out of the stockade. George Emerson, the animal trainer, marveled that he had never heard of a trainer or any other man riding a rhinoceros before. Johnny later confessed that it was easier to ride one than spell it.

And finally, a last genuflection via Weissmuller toward those wacky days when it seemed that anything could happen—this Tarzan business. When else, where else, and how else, could a big, overgrown boy who never had a diction or acting lesson and very little other schooling, make the transition, overnight as it were, from the greatest free-style swimmer the country had ever seen to one of the best-known and -loved moving picture stars in the world?

A pulp writer by the name of Edgar Rice Burroughs, after possibly a slight glance over his shoulder at Mowgli and Co., invented the character that came close to outselling the Bible, and made him a millionaire. M.G.M. bought the rights and went shopping for an actor to play the part of the wild boy grown up in the African jungle. They gave Weissmuller a trial because he stripped so gorgeously, and for the next twelve years, Johnny practically lived up a tree for them. Since the jungle child's English was limited almost to the famous line—"Me Tarzan, you Jane," dialogue presented no problem. Emotions were equally limited. Once lady fans had seen those teeth gleaming from the handsome, swarthy face out of a leafy bower, or that splendid leopard skin-draped torso come hurtling down out of the trees

Johnny with another Golden person, the great backstroke champion Eleanor Holm.

. . . and with his former wife, Lupe Velez.

to where they could get a good look at it, emotions and histrionics ran for Sweeney. That face and that body became as well-known in Outer Mongolia as on Michigan Avenue or Broadway and Forty-second Street.

The money take may have been delayed, for during his nine years of competition, Weissmuller was strictly an amateur and even in those days, nobody was paying swimmers. But the aura, the glitter, and the magic were there just the same and as deservedly as any of the others; Johnny cashed in as a professional. He remains for me one of the truly great ones of those times.

If there isn't a statue of him in the lobby of the Illinois Athletic Club, there ought to be one.

Down out of his tree for a moment, Tarzan and His Mate *with Maureen O'Sullivan playing the mate.*

The most gallant and versatile woman athlete who ever lived—Mildred (Babe) Didrikson Zaharias.

CHAPTER **12**

Babe Didrikson

(1913–1956)

In the chronological sense of this series, and the renaissance of American sports and champions during the great decade, the heroine of this chapter does not belong, for she first appeared upon the scene in 1932 and scored her greatest triumphs at an even later date. But if there ever was a golden person of golden heart and spirit, it was the late Mildred Didrikson Zaharias, the Texas Babe, the most splendid woman athlete of our times.

On every count, accomplishment, temperament, personality, and color, she belongs to the ranks of those story-book champions of our age of innocence. And even in that company she would have been outstanding, not only for her achievements in two such diverse sports as track and field and golf, but for her all-around abilities coupled with an intrinsic grace and unspoiled naturalness, all embodied in one slip of a girl who stood 5 feet 6½ inches and weighed no more than 126 pounds.

You of this present era must indeed accuse me of exaggeration when I say that she was probably the most talented athlete, male or female, ever developed in our country. Yet it is true. In all my years at the sports desk I have never encountered any man who could play as many different games well as did the Babe.

As in the case of Weissmuller, the Associated Press poll in 1950 confirmed this by nominating her as the woman athlete of the first half of the twentieth century. I am convinced that in the year 2000 the grandsons of the pollsters, looking back, may add another fifty years and make her the woman athlete of the

The young Babe from Dallas, before the 1932 Olympics and fame.

Form, speed, and the will to win.

This one with Artie McGovern was posed, but she could box and hit like a middleweight.

entire century, and I would not be surprised if one never saw
her like again.

There is no sport that you can name in which she could not
perform competently and in some cases brilliantly, including
several which are restricted to men such as football, baseball,
boxing, and wrestling. She was a world's champion in track and
field as her Olympic gold medals testify, an All-America basketball player, and a national and international champion in amateur as well as professional golf.

The Babe could run, jump (broad and high), throw the
javelin and the discus, play golf, tennis, polo (water and horse),
basketball, marbles, soccer, lacrosse, billiards; she could dive,
ride, shoot, pitch, bat softball home runs, kick, fence, pass, bowl,
and skate.

And if that isn't enough for you, she was an exquisite ball-
room and adagio dancer, played the harmonica well enough to
be a professional at it, excelled at gin rummy, was a good cook,
and could type a hundred words a minute.

But wait. You haven't heard anything yet. Mildred was a one-
girl track team.

On July 16, 1932, at Evanston, Illinois, in the combined National Women's A. A. U. Track Meet and Olympic tryouts, she
represented Employer's Casualty Co., an insurance firm of
Dallas, Texas, where she worked as a secretary. And that was it,
as far as the Texas firm was concerned. There weren't any other
representatives. By herself, the Babe won the team title with an
aggregate of 30 points. The Illinois Women's Athletic Club, with
a full complement of entrants and competitors in the various
events, finished second to her.

The lone girl from Texas entered eight of the ten scheduled
events. She won the 80-meter hurdles, baseball throw, shotput,
broad jump, and javelin toss, was nosed out of a tie in the high
jump and was fourth in the discus throw. During the course of
that afternoon she set three world's records.

The year before in the National A. A. U. Track and Field
championships, she had compiled an even more amazing record
when she won the 100-yard dash, 80-meter hurdles, 220-yard
dash, javelin, discus, broad and high jumps. She tied for first

place in the 50-yard dash and placed second in the shotput. Out of nine events she took first in eight and second in one.

This wonder child could have been a one-woman Olympic track team as well, except that girls were limited to entries in three events. They must have heard the Babe was coming.

In those '32 Olympics at Los Angeles she won the 80-meter hurdles and the javelin throw and was hornswoggled out of a third gold medal in the high jump when an official, who up to that time had taken no part in the conversation, decided that she was diving over the bar. This decision came when she was tied with Jean Shiley at world record height. She cleared the bar in the jump-off, but was ruled to have dove. Her style had not been questioned prior to this. It is legal today.

Later in life, Babe Didrikson became the greatest woman golf player in the history of the game.

However, if these accomplishments had been her only claim to fame, if she had just been some kind of athletic freak, a skilled technician with natural timing and aptitude for games, she would hardly be remembered with the warmth and affection that fills the hearts of us who knew her. She was a unique and enchanting creature as well—naïve, unspoiled, and honest, who grew into a most splendid and courageous woman. After a struggle that was typical of her lifelong gallantry and fighting spirit, she succumbed to cancer at the age of forty-two.

Great champions are lonely people. Their very uniqueness that sets them upon the pinnacle and the sacrifices they are called upon to make to reach it, cut them off in many ways from their less exalted fellows. For many years until the Babe met and married her big, hearty, and adoring wrestler husband, George Zaharias, she was a pathetic and solitary figure, neither one thing nor another in the average, normal world of ordinary men and women or even, for that matter, of athletes.

She was described as the tomboy to end all tomboys, and yet underneath she was wistful, childlike, and soft-hearted, and her "upping" to opponents to drawl, "Ahm gonna whup you," was nothing but a cover for a girl who, in her formative years, thought she was too plain to compete for boys and who therefore became a boy herself, though only superficially, decrying the frivolous or feminine and taking it out upon her sex by "whupping" them in everything else.

Had the Babe rocketed across our skies ten years earlier she too would have been ticker-tape blizzarded up Broadway, bussed by Grover Whalen, and inundated with money offers. She would have become a part of the million-dollar splurge.

Marvelous Mildred was just too late for this, for the party was over. The stock market had crashed and we were in the throes of the big disillusionment, our innocence despoiled. Last night's millionaires were tomorrow morning's corpses on the sidewalk, beneath their skyscraping offices. Financial wizards became apple-peddling mendicants. Santa Claus, it developed, was in truth nothing but an old bum dressed in a red suit and whiskers, tinkling his bell over the Salvation Army collection pot. And the architect of World War II was already strutting across the map of Germany.

It was as though a sponge had been passed across a slate, wiping out everything that had been written thereon. Our interest in sports survived, but the passion, the fire, and the dedication was no more and not again would we escape so wholeheartedly into the never-never land of the heroes and heroines of our games. From then on we had other worries.

Babe Didrikson's two fabulous performances in the Women's A.A.U. meets of 1931 and 1932 did not rate more than a stick or two in the metropolitan press. She made good copy with her Olympic victories in Los Angeles, but more as a curiosity because of her boyish appearance and sometimes even as a cruel joke, such as went the rounds of the sportswriters out there at the time, that when she went to play golf there was some question as to whether to send her to the men's or the women's locker room. Ten years before there would have been a queue of promoters lined up to exploit her sensational diversity of talents.

If the public now was inclined to be apathetic, the professionals were less so. After the Games, Babe Didrikson, Olin Dutra (pro at the Los Angeles Country Club), the late Grantland Rice and myself teamed up in a foursome to see whether it was true about the Babe's golf game.

On the first tee she "upped" to the ball very quietly, glanced down the fairway, and after but one preliminary waggle, lashed out a 260-yard drive.

Rice gasped, "Did you see that?"

Dutra replied, "I saw it but I don't believe it!"

That day she played the second nine in forty-three. It was only her eleventh game of golf, nor had she ever had a lesson.

This was also the match which demonstrated to me the competitive guile of a horny-handed veteran lodged in the person of an eighteen-year-old infant. Rice was paired with Didrikson. With Dutra to support my own staggering game, we came up to the short, par 3, sixteenth hole one up. By one of those quirks of golf, Rice, Didrikson, and Dutra were off line. Gallico, the dub was on the green ten feet from the pin. The match ought to have been in the bag.

The Babe said to me, "Race you to the green!"

I fell. We belted down the arroyo and up the hill, Didrikson staying within reach just enough to keep me interested and letting me win the race to collapse, gasping and trembling on the greensward, thereafter to take four putts, two of them from within a foot.

The Babe—she was actually *named* Mildred Babe Didrikson —was of Norwegian extraction. Her father was a ship's carpenter who retired from the sea to Port Arthur, Texas where she was born, one of seven children. Later they moved to Beaumont and finally to Dallas.

Even as a child, Mildred was a tomboy and anti-feminine. She never played with dolls and in fact had some kind of block where such toys were concerned. One time during the '32 Olympics when I asked if there was anything that she *didn't* play, she replied, "Yea, dolls."

She had a thing about the word "sissy" too, and when I first met and learned to know her she lumped all matters feminine, such as makeup, hairdressers, seductive clothing, and girls who indulged in them under that word. And once, when interviewed about her marriage aims or ambitions, she made a point of declaring that her husband mustn't be sissy. In three-hundred-pound professional wrestler George Zaharias, whom she married in 1938, she found her mate. Whatever else one could say about

She played championship basketball.

She could pitch like a man.

Anything she tried, she could do.

But golf was her favorite game and she compiled a championship record which may never be equaled. Here she is applying body English to a putt.

wrestlers, and there was plenty being said in those days, they were certainly no sissies.

All of this was, of course, wholly defensive, for the Babe was far from being a beauty when first we laid eyes on her at the old Wardman Park Hotel in Los Angeles, where the Olympic women's team was quartered.

I can see her today as vividly as I did then. She looked as though she had been cut out of rawhide leather, with sand-colored hair, lively gray-green eyes, straight mouth, thin-lipped in a hatchet face set upon a long neck featured by a prominent Adam's apple. There was a fuzz on her upper lip and hair on her strong, muscular legs. Lookswise it had been her fate to enter the gawky stage earlier, remain longer, and emerge later than most girls. But during that period she turned herself into the physical marvel that made everyone forget her lack of beauty.

Yet I remember how even then she touched my heart and made an impression upon me. And I was supposed to be a callous, tough sportswriter from New York. She was certainly unlike any girl I had ever seen before, this apparently hard-boiled tomboy. But it was not too difficult to catch a glimpse of something warm, brave, and perhaps even hurt, struggling like a chrysalis to emerge from a cocoon.

And, of course, the loneliness was so evident. I remember well the evening before the Babe's events in the Olympics. There was a garden party on the lawn of the Wardman Park and the kids were skylarking—Georgia Coleman, Joan McSheehey, and lovely Eleanor Holm with a group of the men swimmers and divers. Somehow it went into a kind of aimless round dance, hands joined. The circle swept past where Didrikson was standing watching, clad in her blue track overalls with the U.S. shield on her breast.

The blond and handsome Coleman broke the circle, ran to her, and cried, "Come on, Babe! Get in with us. We're having a Paul Jones."

Babe replied, "Aw shoot, honey, Ah cain't. Ah'm competin' tomorrow . . . Ah cain't play tonight."

They joined hands again and went on without her, a circle of young, gay, laughing faces, leaving her segregated by her ambition.

Never before had nature lavished such gifts of timing and gamesmanship upon any one woman. In her first game of local, tournament basketball she scored forty points and from 1929 to 1931, she led the Dallas Cyclones to three national championships and was twice named All-America forward.

Playing in Houston, she attracted the attention of Colonel M. J. McCombs, himself a former athlete, who persuaded her to take a job as a typist with his Dallas insurance firm and there coached her in running, jumping, hurdling, and field sports. Babe never went back on him and later, when everyone was trying to get into the act and take credit for her skills, she stated firmly, "Shoot, they's just one man coached me and that's Colonel McCombs."

But where did she learn all the other things she could do; to rifle the 5 ball into the corner pocket, sling a football, whip a baseball 296 feet, twist herself off a ten-foot board in the two and a half gainer, a difficult one even for men? Or throw a straight right (fooling around, she once split light-heavyweight Bill Stribling's lip), parry and riposte like lightning with a foil, send a strike down the alley and crack a polo ball half the length of the field? No one really knows or remembers, except that this was nature's gift to her. Whatever game she tried came easy to her and she solved its basic problems after a few attempts.

Thus, she could have become a champion and an enduring star at anything upon which she chose to concentrate. When the A.A.U., in one of its classic blunders, turned her into a professional because some product had used her picture without her permission, she decided upon golf, stayed out of competition until she had regained her amateur status, practicing and perfecting herself all the while, and then over the following years became the world's best.

The tomboy disappeared forever and Mrs. Mildred Zaharias, golf champion, competitor, and wife, emerged in an image of grace and accomplishment which never during a single moment of her career was tarnished.

And the transition from the man-girl who hated sissies to a feminine woman, confident of herself as such, took place in a

few years' time. It was after the '32 Olympics that I met Babe
again, at the Men's National Open golf championship at Pittsburgh. And she was "sis" from her head to her toes, her hair
waved, lips and cheeks touched up, stylish sports clothes, and
initialed handbag completely equipped for repairs, with comb,
compact, lipstick, and lace handkerchief.

She caught my look of surprise and admiration and grinned
at me. She must have read those early pieces I had written about
her, for she hitched up her skirt just enough to show the elegant
slip underneath. "It's silk," she said, "and Ah like it."

And so in her chosen sport of golf she concentrated on her
play and went on to rack up a record which like all our other
greats of the long ago has never been equaled. She won the U. S.
Women's Amateur and All-America Open; she was the first
American to win the British Women's Amateur title; she was a
three-time winner of the world's championship at Tam ọ' Shanter, and set an all-time record the seasons of 1946–47 by winning
seventeen straight tournaments. From 1935, when she began her
active golfing career, until 1953 when felled by cancer, she won
a total of eighty-two tournaments.

So had the times changed, however, that hardly any of us
were aware of the last and most tremendous physical and spiritual achievement of this sports champion. In the spring of 1953
she won the Babe Zaharias tournament, named after her. Ten
days later she entered a hospital in Beaumont, Texas and was
operated on for cancer. The operation, dangerous and excruciat-
ing, is known as a colostomy and it left her no longer a whole or
normal person.

It would have stopped anyone but the Babe. Three and a half
months later she was back competing in the All-American at the
Tam o' Shanter, in the midsummer heat of Chicago, and actually
took third place. Six months after this she won the five-thousand-
dollar Serbin Women's Invitational Tournament at Miami Beach,
and in 1954 captured the National Women's Open *and* the Tam
o' Shanter All-American as well.

It took the recurring cancer to vanquish her. In 1955 she was
hospitalized again. Her golf clubs were kept in a corner of the
sick room where her eyes could rest upon them to help her in the

When this picture was taken after winning a golf tournament held in her honor at Beaumont, Texas, Mrs. Zaharias was already stricken with cancer.

hopeless fight. For fight she did until the very last day, when she passed away in her sleep with her husband at her side. These were her greatest hours, as athlete, woman, and human being.

The nation paused for one brief second to note that she was no more, but it was only we who had known her as the sissy-hating hoyden and Texas tomboy of the '32 Olympic Games, and her subsequent rise, who remembered how truly marvelous she was and that, born ten years too late, she belonged really to our galaxy of the super men and women of the Golden Decade.

"Any ice today, ma'am?" Harold (Red) Grange, *the Wheaton iceman, also known as The Galloping Ghost of the Illini.*

CHAPTER **13**

Red Grange

H

e had the name for it!

Red Grange!

Say it to yourself—"Red Grange, Red Grange, Red Grange!"

The combination had a swing and lilt to it. Add a thatch of red hair on a 5-foot 10-inch, 170-pound body in moleskins, an orange number 77 on a blue jersey, and a leather helmet; give him the ball to carry and it wanted a row of Sherman tanks to stop him.

And this being the pre-Sherman tank era of 1923–25, it was: "Look out, here he comes! Hell, there he goes!"

During that period, Red Grange, halfback of the University of Illinois, ran wild through, around, and over some of the best football teams in the country. He was the player of the era.

Knute Rockne's Four Horsemen left their imprint upon the Golden Decade of the 1920s but they were a backfield, working with well-gauged and machine-like precision. Grange was an individual, and his accomplishments and influence are all the more remarkable when it is considered that the public life of a varsity man in college is limited to three years. Nobody hears of him as a freshman, and after graduation he disappears either into business or professional football.

In those days the pro game had not yet acquired the standing and following of today and was even somehow faintly discreditable, tied up to squads with strange names and places such as the Canton Bulldogs, or the Something-or-Other Yellow Jackets. Indeed when Grange decided, in his senior year, to cash in upon his sensational amateur performances and signed up

His hair was flaming red.

Here he comes!
There he goes!

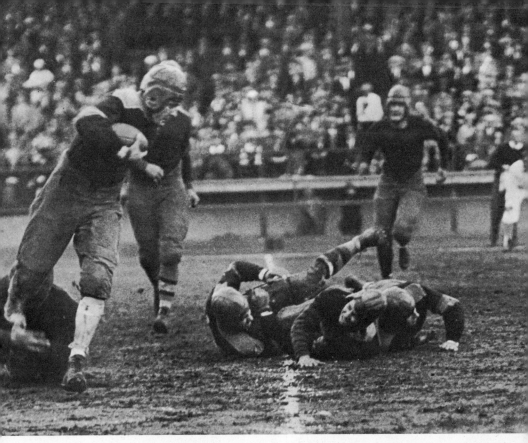

Slippery as an eel. He got away for sixty yards on this one.

with a professional promoter, a shudder ran through the ranks
of the universities as though he had backslid from the church.

To me, one of the most fascinating things in retrospect about
the era with which this book is concerned, is the extent of the
impudence of bodies governing amateur sports. From the moment they began to lay their hands on some real cash, and thus
became professionals themselves, they went into a perfect tizzy
about amateurism for no practical purpose that I can see, even
today, but to hog all of the loot. If the football stars who were
developing through the upgrading of the game in importance
and intersectionalism, had asked for a percentage of the big
money they were drawing, there would have been a howl heard
from coast to coast.

It is an interesting irony that Grange, who was 100 per cent
amateur and gratis player, should in a way have been instru-

Football turns boys into men.

mental in the eventual corruption of hundreds of colleges and universities. It is estimated that during Red's university day an aggregate of some eight hundred thousand spectators paid their way into college stadia to see him play, let us say at an average of two dollars a ticket, and we have Grange responsible for pulling in $1,600,000 at the gate, of which his share was a football uniform, some meals at a training table, and possibly some tuition 'paid. It is true the universities were building and maintaining huge stadia to accommodate the crowds now clamoring to see the games, but those must be considered a part of public relations and promotion for the schools, useful in wheedling grants and donations out of satisfied alumni.

Nor does the irony end here. For in their frantic attempts to acquire similar attractions, the universities impaled themselves front, back, and sideways on the horns of the dilemma that had been created—how to coax, lure, rent, hire, or buy football stars who would be drawing cards, while at the same time managing to keep their fingers off the swag. During this process they fractured amateur codes into so many pieces that no one has yet been able to put them together again.

Statisticians vary as to Grange's lifetime record, but the one generally accepted is that through his playing days in high school, college, and professional football, he took part in 237 games, carried the ball 4013 times for an average of 8.1 yards, or more than 18 miles, and scored some 531 touchdowns. His career lasted 13 years.

It was he more than any one single individual who boosted college football from what up to that time had been little more than an afternoon's airing for one's coonskin coat, girl, hip flask and a big, yellow chrysanthemum, into a million-dollar industry, amateur and professional, and which is still growing to this day.

Once more, as so often in that lush period, the man and the money achieved the magical figures. Harold Edward Grange, born June 13, 1903, son of the small-town police chief in Wheaton, Illinois, was definitely one of the elect.

And like all of those extraordinary personages, his contribution was not only to his sport, but he was thoroughly a product of his times and his impact was upon our imaginations. Grange was the great escape artist and in the illusory world of fiction in which all of us were living, he represented the good guy, the quarry in the pursuit. He was the man millions of people hoped would get away.

Now, the chase was something purely American and was brought to its highest pinnacle through the streets of a Los Angeles suburb called Hollywood and the moving picture studios located there. Charlie Chaplin, Buster Keaton, Harold Lloyd fled from villainous pursuers; Douglas Fairbanks, Sr. contrived incredible escapes from hordes of evildoers; Mack Sennett cops ran riot all over the place, and no Western was complete without good men and bad, hounding one another over the Hollywood hills.

The pattern of entertainment had been established, and Red Grange was the slippery eel who transferred this comedy melodrama to the football field as he eluded the arms, grasping fingers, and clutching hands of burly tacklers by twos and threes, who tried to whipsaw him high and low, drive him out of bounds or into pockets. He was the Artful Dodger of the century, and people went wild with excitement and delight watching him do it.

His progress was not so much a swift, breathless speeding as it was a threading, a picking his way through the throng of defenders, like a harried suburbanite dodging through the station crush, carrying a package containing something that might spoil if he failed to make the 5:33. It was his change of pace, sometimes almost imperceptible from the stands, which would throw a tackler off balance and give Red an extra fraction of a second to get by. He had the speed too, when it was wanted, and when he was in the clear. On defense he could eat up yardage and pull a man down from behind like a jaguar clawing an antelope.

He was a touchdown factory, just as Babe Ruth was home run dispenser or Bob Jones a birdie machine. And as such he afforded moments of illimitable pride and satisfaction to hundreds of thousands of spectators who, in one way or another, were connected with the University of Illinois, or later simply were Midwestern rooters.

College football was then, and probably is still, an extension of our egos and aggressive wishes to triumph over our rivals, and we have seen how the University of Notre Dame acquired adherents and Subway Alumni who had never been near the school, but who identified themselves with "The Fighting Irish" and Notre Dame's success.

Red Grange was the instrument or the spokesman for the Illini and all of their adherents, and as his fame and scores mounted, he became truly the vicarious muscle of the Midwest. In his weekly quotas of dramatic runs and scores two set pieces stand out as unforgettable:

The first of these was the miraculous day against Michigan in 1924, when in twelve minutes against a team forecast as the best of the Big Ten Conference that year, he scored four touchdowns, on runs of 92, 70, 57, and 43 yards. Withdrawn from the game at the end of the first quarter completely exhausted from the sheer running, never mind the bumps and knocks, 70,000 spectators gave him a five-minute standing ovation, one of the greatest ever accorded an athlete. Not content with this, Grange reappeared in the third quarter, ran another 64 yards for a fifth touchdown, and threw a forward pass for the sixth.

More sensational still, however, in my opinion, was Grange's performance against the University of Pennsylvania in 1925.

For all Red's astonishing record, he was still a Midwestern phenomenon. He had not yet convinced the East. As fate decreed, Illinois had scheduled a game with Penn that year, and the Philadelphians were unbeaten and untied, numbering Yale, Brown, and Chicago among their victims, while the Westerners had lost three of their big games.

Pennsylvania was ready and loaded for Grange. And if ever a stage was set for a highly touted, two-time All-American and possibly overrated football hero to fall on his face, it was that October afternoon in Franklin Field, Philadelphia, before a capacity crowd of 60,000.

Further to hamper a player who depended upon his footwork, it had rained that morning and the ground was sloppy.

And so the first time Red Grange carried the ball from scrimmage, from his own 44-yard line, after a preliminary exchange of punts, he went through left tackle 56 yards for a touchdown.

This chips-down performance must rank with the called home

run of Babe Ruth, the tipped-off steals of Ty Cobb, Tilden's danger-line tennis, and the Jones' pursuit of four major titles in one year. This *was* delivering the goods. Also there was nothing stingy about Grange, for in that game he set up Illinois' next tally with a long runback off Pennsylvania's second kick-off, and scored two more touchdowns on scampers of 13 and 20 yards. Illinois won 24–2, and the redhead had proved his point. From then on he was a national idol.

There was nothing about the pre-teenage Grange to indicate that here was yet another of the Golden People, and no one has yet penetrated into the prodigality of that exceptional time, or the mystery of the particular arrangement of cells and molecules which were to enable one boy to run, twist, dodge, evade, and score more frequently than any other before or since.

One of Grange's most endearing qualities, and which helped to mark him as the All-American boy as well as player, was his modesty. Interviewed by sportswriters after one of his sensational performances, he referred to the assistance he had had from his blockers, as well as the fact that coach Bob Zuppke's plays were designed to shake him loose.

Good blocking he did have. Zuppke's plays were indeed built around Red's abilities. But what must not be forgotten is that when offense is designed for one of those fancy-stepping, hip-swiveling fellows, the opposition coaches who have had plenty of time to scout him, rearrange their defenses and theirs is the simpler problem—a matter of concentrating upon one character. They know he will try to get loose sooner or later, and it is simply a question of covering him properly.

For instance, when Red Cagle, another carrot-top with a nice, loose motion, was galloping wild for Army, the defense solved him very quickly and eventually he was found doing more running back and forth behind his own forwards than toward the goal line, and a couple of times I thought they were going to chase him clear out of the stadium by the back door.

Not so Red Harold. They knew he was coming; they saw him start; he made no secret of his direction; he was in their midst; and he was gone! At times you would have thought him some kind of wizard, invisibly enmagicked and protected by spells, so easily and helplessly did the would-be tacklers slide off from his inviolate person. No wonder that this exceptional artistry enthralled the imagination of a sports-mad country, and won him the nickname of The Galloping Ghost.

Grange's early history could be produced in a nutshell: At Wheaton High School in his junior year he averaged five touchdowns a game. By graduation time every Midwestern football coach had his eye on him. Admiration for Bob Zuppke led him to Illinois where, unimpressed by his own record and in the face of the stars gathered there, Red was shy about trying out until, as a freshman halfback, a 65-yard run through the entire varsity team persuaded himself, Zuppke, and everyone else that he was no fluke. The season of 1923, as a sophomore, Harold Red Grange flamed like a shooting star across the football sky. Take a look at his record.

But there is no explanation of the built-in ability of this singular boy.

There is none, for that matter, for any of these extraordinary people—freaks of nature, if you will—and still less for the fact that so many of them seemed to make their appearance almost simultaneously during that ten-year span. To us who were so close to it, it did not seem all that unusual at the time. Only when we had left the twenties and embarked into the thirties did it become apparent that we had just passed through a most remarkable phase of development in both amateur and professional sports in the United States. Hundreds of top-class football players, kickers, passers, and broken-field runners, capable of breaking loose for the touchdown, have come upon the scene since then—and vanished, too. But the name that is still remembered wherever football is discussed, is that of Red Grange.

He was human—well, almost—and had his off day or days. He was forced to sit out a number of games through injuries since, when the members of the opposition did catch up with him, it was considered their duty to try to break his leg, or provide him with some kind of permanent incapacity when they threw him down. His worst season was 1925, when he went scoreless in four games out of seven. But all this was forgotten because of his magnificent wiping of the eye of the East against Pennsylvania.

And with anyone but Grange, one would hardly call 1213 yards gained running and 119 accounted for by 15 passes, a bad season.

Grange may have had some minor scholarship assistance to aid him in paying his tuition at Illinois, but he was an eminently honest and 100 per cent amateur player. During the summer months he worked delivering ice in his home town of Wheaton, earning both money and the sobriquet, "The Wheaton Iceman."

But although he remained an amateur at heart and in fact during his college days, Red was no fool. A sensible, loyal, straightforward boy, he played out his prodigious string for the University of Illinois "on the house," as it were, but after his final game against Ohio State in 1925 in which, although he did not figure in the scoring, his running and passing were responsible for victory, he was ready to shake the golden tree.

He announced coolly that he was out to make a million dollars.

Twenty-four hours after he had turned in his sweat-stained No. 77 jersey to Coach Zuppke, Grange sent shudders through the ranks of the you-play-for-nothing-but-we-rake-in-the-coin people by signing a contract to be managed by C. C. Pyle, as well as to play for George Halas of the Chicago Bears.

Pyle himself deserves a niche in this waxworks of the twenties. He could have been invented and played by the late W. C. Fields. But he was a flesh-and-blood person and the creator of the famous transcontinental marathon foot race, or Bunion Derby as it was nicknamed. This was a concept as cruel, grotesque, and striking as the dance marathons. A horde of professional runners competing for a money prize raced across the 3000 miles of continent in stages of 15 to 20 miles a day, pausing at night for sleep and jogging on the next morning. C. C. Pyle got his out of advertising displayed by the caravan and fees paid by towns and villages for routing his masochist ragtag mob down their main streets.

Just as an example of the drawing power of Grange, on Sunday, December 6, 1925, some 73,651 souls jammed their way into the Polo Grounds in New York, the largest crowd it had ever held before or since. Its added capacity resulted from the fact that extra seats had been installed for the Army-Navy game the previous week. This was to see Grange in a 19–7 Bear victory over the New York Giants. Up to that time attendance of 18,000 or so was about tops for the pros.

Before the year was out Red had cashed in close to half a million dollars on his name, in one way or another, and in 1926 and 1927, under Pyle's management, he drew a million into the box office.

For the next ten years Grange continued to pull them in. And the truly remarkable sidelight to the professional career of this phenomenal young man is that during this time he learned to be a football player, which is something quite different from a tricky broken-field runner. The pros, anyway, have a tendency to smother and discourage those lone ball-carriers. Red became a great pass receiver as well as passer, a kicker and a first-class defensive back, an adept diagnoser of quick-breaking enemy plays. In short, from having been a sensational and certainly most publicized individual star of all time, he changed into the kind of team player necessary to the strategy of Bear Coach Halas.

He did more than this for the professional sport. He attracted hundreds of thousands of new fans by the magic attached to his name and number. They saw not only the famous Galloping Ghost at work, but also a totally different kind of football than they had ever seen before; a game so refined by study and practice and hence far removed from the often ineptness of college teams, that the foundation was laid for its great and deserved popularity today.

Yet it will be to those three years when Grange wore the big "77" of Illinois between his shoulder blades, to which the old-timers will wish to hark back in their memories and I, too, will join them there. For the thrill of big-time college football was then still new to us, and the jam-packed stadia with their crowds of from sixty to ninety thousand spectators, their quota of fresh-faced, clear-eyed, lovely girls clad in autumn colors, were stimulating and marvelous to us.

In our ears rings the echo of cheers rolling over the players-for-free; we see again the college bands parading, the leaping, white-sweatered cheerleaders, and feel the electric atmosphere

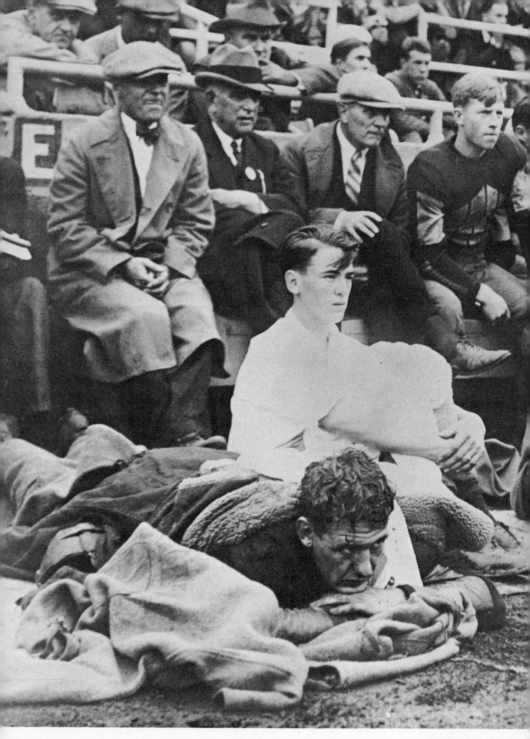

He played with all his heart and soul and when he was sidelined through exhaustion, he shed tears.

of youth. And above all, we remember that wizard, red-haired young man sweeping us to our feet with his elegant eluding, avoiding and side-stepping, whipping the huge stadium to a screaming pitch of hysterical excitement as, spinning like a tee-totum from one hairbreadth escape to another, he climaxed his poetically rhythmic run with a touchdown. This was part of a light-hearted, carefree existence of which not too much in gaiety and delight seems to linger on.

The champion of champions and the greatest gentleman of them all—
Robert Tyre Jones.

CHAPTER **14**

Bob Jones

There is a picture that remains embedded in the recesses of memory, of a locker room of a country club in Minneapolis, late on a steamy, hundred-degree, humid afternoon of July 1930 and a gang, some with towels about their middles, sitting around relaxing after the day's play.

The occasion was rather a serious one. The club was Interlachen, the play had been for the U. S. National Open championship, and it had been won by Bobby Jones who, previously that year, had captured the British Amateur and the British Open.

Somebody asked the chunky little man nursing the Georgia Corn-and-branch, "What are you going to do when you retire, Bob?"

There was a moist and mischievous gleam in the champion's eye from the soothing effects of his first drink during the four grueling days of the tournament and, grinning, he turned to another who was likewise celebrating with sour mash and said, "You'd better tell them, O.B.—you know."

O. B. Keeler, golf writer for the Atlanta *Journal*, lifelong, intimate friend and Boswell to Jones, fastened his towel securely around his loins and arising, sonorously declaimed from memory the lines of Hilaire Belloc:

> If I ever become a rich man,
> Or if ever I grow to be old,
> I will build a house with a deep thatch
> To shelter me from the cold,
> I will hold my house in the high woods
> Within a walk of the sea,
> And the men that were boys when I was a boy
> Shall sit and drink with me.

And when he had thus recited, the new champion got up and joined him; the two men put their arms about one another's shoulders and chorused the last two lines in unison, swept an exaggerated bow, hoisted their glasses once more, and serious drinking was resumed.

Later on, when the locker room had almost emptied, Jones, his father "the Colonel," O. B. Keeler, the late Grantland Rice and a few others, lingered on for some quartet singing, heads together in deep harmony and from behind the rows of steel lockers one heard the strains of:

> Honey, honey bless yo' h'aht,
> Mah honey that Ah loves so well,

missing out on none of the lovely, barber shop swipes.

In this vignette is much that was best, memorable, and likable about Robert Tyre Jones, Jr., who, on that particular day, was three legs up on his incredible journey to his Grand Slam effort of winning the British Open, the British Amateur, the U. S. Open, and the U. S. Amateur all in one year. He was the finest golfer and competitor ever produced in the United States, or anywhere else, the King himself of the Golden People.

We have seen two of our heroes of yesteryear, Ruth and Cobb, calling their shots at some portion of a single ball game and then delivering the goods. Jones called his on the Grand Slam, except that only two people knew it—his father and Keeler. Yet, Jones started the year 1930 with both the hope and expectation of winning the four major championships. His modesty shines through his reason for not making his intentions public: "I felt reluctant to admit that I considered myself capable of such an accomplishment."

And if by now you are not fed to the teeth with superlatives, stay with me, I beg of you, for this closing session of the Old Codgers' or Beard-Mumblers' Club. I would like to tell you a little something about the man who, of all those I met and knew during my fourteen years as a sportswriter, spanning 1922 through 1936, impressed me as being the best sportsman, the greatest gentleman, and the champion of champions.

When I knew him and tagged at his heels as a reporter, he was a stockily built young fellow of medium height, with sandy-brown hair and a pleasant, open face. Again, he stripped not like an athlete, but an ordinary man in good trim with no visible musculature. He had a warm, all-embracing grin and a fine, derisory expression about his eyes and mouth when telling one against himself. He had the gift of laughter and self-ridicule. He enjoyed a drink, a funny story, and companionship, and had an enviable and fluent repertoire with which to correct the line of a ball in flight.

He was that rare person, a genuine amateur, in a time when the whole concept of amateurism in the United States was being shattered. He loved golf for the fun of it, the fellowship of the foursome, the jokes, the lies at handicapping time, the scrapping and struggling to win a dollar Nassau. And there was more truth than childish ignorance to the anecdote that when he was a boy and going around the Eastlake course with his father, he asked, "Dad, what do people do who don't play golf on Sunday?"

A part of Jones was that warm and amusing relationship he had with his parent. Bob preferred to play with the old gentleman more than with anyone else because, as he said, "Dad used to get so mad." "The Colonel," of course, was taking perpetual golf lessons from his famous son. Jones, Sr. always appeared in the galleries of Jones, Jr.

I remember that final day at the Merion Country Club at Ardmore, Pennsylvania where Jones completed the Slam by winning the U. S. Amateur championship. A group of us, Colonel Jones, O. B. Keeler, Chick Ridley, and a mess of writers, were standing on a hillside with field glasses, like generals in an old print, watching Jones and his opponent Gene Homans coming up to the green of the long fourth, the afternoon of the 36-hole finals.

The distant, tiny figure of Jones stepped up to the ball and seemed merely to wave his arms. It climbed into the sky and sailed to the pin.

"My word, Colonel," said Grantland Rice, "your boy almost strained himself to death hitting that one!"

"I wasn't looking at him hitting it," said father Jones, "I was looking at that sign that boy is carrying. It says, 'JONES NINE UP.' Man, that's the finest-looking sign I ever saw."

The game's most perfect form.

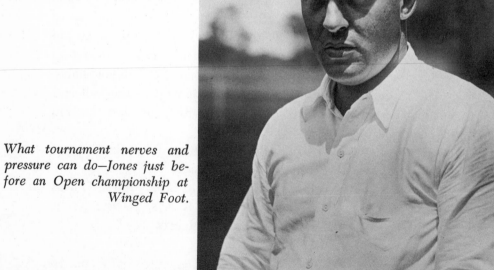

What tournament nerves and pressure can do—Jones just before an Open championship at Winged Foot.

At ease, playing out of the rough in a charity match.

The game, for the duffer who competes in no more than an occasional club handicap, is probably the least strenuous physically, and visually the least dramatic sport of any, and is recommended by the medical profession to old gaffers with too much suet collecting around their middles. But to my generation Jones was the be-all and end-all of this royal and ancient pastime, the Grand Panjandrum, the mighty wizard, warlock, shaman, high priest, the Great God Golf himself. Thousands of people followed him when he played in the hope as well as quite possibly belief, that if they only watched him play or were near him, some of his magic would rub off onto them.

Like every other sport, golf enjoyed an explosive boom in the 1920s. Five years before that date it was estimated that there were no more than a quarter of a million addicts in the country, half a million by 1920, and ten years later at least five million trying to control that pesky little white ball.

The explanation for this was: more leisure time, more money, more golf courses, and—Jones.

The popularity and publicity attained by this modest young Southerner, born in Atlanta, Georgia on St. Patrick's Day 1902, set an entire nation golf-crazy. Membership in a country club became practically obligatory for status. The ritual of the Sunday morning foursome was almost more rigid than church attendance. And as the final accolade of arrival, the low handicap golfer could get himself a cushy job as a customer's man with any brokerage house or Wall Street concern, with duties no more onerous than playing a round or two with a visiting moneybag and murmuring, "Oh, good shot, sir!" when same connected with a ball which landed anywhere within bounds.

These elements and the worship of Jones tied in with the fact that golf was a game that everyone of every age could play. It had been blessed by the doctors and was healthful. One did not have to be endowed with muscles or more than ordinary coordination. In the playing of it one was not hit, stabbed, bruised, or knocked down and, best of all, the ball was not thrown. It remained immobile, giving one a chance to get set to take a swipe at it. Everywhere municipalities were constructing public links, and anyone who could afford the price of a set of mallets could join in the fun.

True, there were some complications in that the golf swing was not a natural one and the ball showed irritating tendencies to fly off at tangents and come to rest in unwholesome parts of the landscape. But there were professionals galore to initiate beginners into the hang of the thing, and after a few lessons away they would go, happily hacking and blasting.

And Jones, the amateur, was our boy—the shining star in the sky that beckoned us on. If we couldn't all be Dempseys, Tildens,

Weissmullers, or Red Granges, we could—at least occasionally—
vicariously experience the glory that was Jones when, by sheer
accident, we managed to put together three good shots in a row
and rack up a bird on a par 4 hole.

We were Jones and Jones was us, because all through his career
he was the only one who really behaved like the ordinary, everyday golfer who attended to his job and played at weekends. His
business then was to grow up and acquire an education. During
some of his greatest tournament years he was at Georgia Tech
and later Harvard Law School, and in 1928 was admitted to the
Bar. He could do all this and still go up to an Open championship and wipe the eyes of professionals of the caliber of Walter
Hagen, Gene Sarazen, Tommy Armour, Bob Cruickshank, the
Smiths, Horton and MacDonald, Leo Diegel, Johnny Farrell, and
others of that class.

This filled us with all of the naughty boy's glee experienced
when teacher falls on his face in front of the class, and everybody
felt a share in these triumphs.

The tremendous satisfaction it afforded us, our gratitude and
the affection we felt for him exploded upon his return from
abroad, after he had won the British Amateur and the British
Open consecutively and reached the halfway mark on his journey
to the Grand Slam. We did not even know at the time that he was
after it, but no American ever before had won the two big British
titles in the same year and so we gave him "the treatment"; the
ticker-tape ride up Broadway just as we had to Ederle, Lindbergh, and others.

Aboard the city tug *Macom,* Grover Whalen snatched Jones
off his liner at Quarantine, ferried him to The Battery, plunked
him into a cavalcade of cars, and drove him up Broadway through
the blizzard of torn-up paper to be received by Mayor Walker.
Today, I doubt whether a similar feat by an American on the
golf course, that is to say the winning of the two British championships, would manage to break out of the sports pages up onto
page one, much less instigate a traffic-stopping delirium. But
that's what we were like then and what Jones meant to us.

Bob Jones was a born golfer. Everything about the game suited
his body, his character, and his competitive spirit. Chromosomes

*The club is through; the ball is on its way, but the Jones head is still
down. Golfers take note!*

must have been collecting in ancestors down through the ages to
produce this curious young man who, at the age of seven, when
other kids were running about playing baseball, was swinging a
lone golf club for hours in imitation of a Scottish professional by
the name of Stuart Maiden, whom he watched giving lessons
at the Eastlake Club in Atlanta. This same boy at the age of
twelve posted a card on the club bulletin board, "Out in 36,
back in 34," tying the amateur record for the course.

Maiden took him in hand, taught and developed him, but his

swing, timing, and pivot were gifts from the gods, the most perfect combined action the game has ever known. Where every other man and woman has had to struggle against the illogicality of a right-handed person having to hit the ball a backhanded stroke with the *left hand,* with Jones it was wholly natural and comfortable from the very beginning. He whistled that clubhead through the ball and dropped the missile on target two hundred yards away.

But the gods, though lavish, first had to have their little joke. Thus, in addition, they bestowed upon him the ambition of a perfectionist and the temper of a mandrill. He passed through seven hellish teenage years losing tournament after tournament from sheer petulance, throwing clubs and even once quitting under fire, until in the end he beat those fun-loving but always jealous Olympians at their own game by developing an enchanting sense of humor and learning to master himself.

From that time on, which was the year 1922, when he tied for second after Gene Sarazen in the Open at Skokie, he was never out of the spotlight, never without some major title through 1930. After his Grand Slam, which he felt he could never hope to duplicate, he retired quietly into the wings and brought our fabulous era to a close.

Jones was probably the only championship competitor who ever came near to being loved out of winning many of the titles which studded his brilliant career.

Even his opponents universally liked and admired him, and the reason for this lay in the nature of the game itself, which inspires all those who indulge in it with affection. Jones played so beautifully, he was such a joy to watch in action—the quiet elegance and smooth rhythm of his stroke, the arc and pattern of the flight of his ball, that he reached the hearts of even the sourest or most misanthropic old pros. And, too, as a sportsman and strict interpreter of the rules, he was a credit to their game. He called strokes upon himself which cost him important tournaments, when the ball had moved no more than the width of an eyelash while addressing it, and no one but himself had seen it.

But to return to this love business, Jones had millions of worshipers—amateur duffers whose flag he was carrying into every tournament and who were rooting for him to win.

And then there were his personal friends from Atlanta of which there were so many, and friends of his father and family, and friends of friends who doted on him and turned up at his tournaments to follow him in the gallery through every hole, exuding worry, pride, and affection. The looks they cast upon him were moist, benign, and misty with adoration, their voices bated and caressing, their attitudes maddeningly adulating to a man who was trying to keep sharp his competitive edge.

They put upon him such a burden of love that he fairly staggered under it and turned sick with nerves and the pressure of trying to win, not for himself but for them, and not to let down the side. This over and above the yahoos he did not even know, who came galumphing after him between tee and green to shout, "I've got a big bet on you, Bobby boy!"—or more likely, "Bobby lad." And how Jones hated to be called "Bobby" and "lad." He was "Bob" to his intimates.

Anyone who has played any kind of a game knows that there is nothing that so stimulates the winning spirit as a little bit of underdogism or hatred, to get a competitor's back up to the point where he produces that extra championship something to turn the trick. Consider yourself, now, in Jones' plight, suffocating in treacly waves of affection and well-wishing, carrying the load of everyone's goodwill and prayers and back-patting and this in a game which, while not physically grueling, is in other ways the most nerve-racking and finicky in the world.

In medal play Jones could not even work up a grudge against an opponent. His sole enemies were himself and the landscape; friendly, smiling nature, lush grass, beautiful, spreading trees, silvery babbling brooks. Even the rude, irresponsible gallery was a paradox, for while its bad manners, insensitivity, and monstrous lack of consideration were a constant and harrying handicap, it was nonetheless composed of adoring people who were just like overgrown, uncontrollable, lolloping, and slobbering puppy dogs.

This was one of the problems that Jones had to overcome and did, along with the other hazards of the game.

Jones' winning of the four major championships of Great

Britain and America, the Grand Slam, has probably had more words written about it than any other sporting event, for the odds against such a feat were astronomical.

And one of the most interesting features of these odds was that they were not entirely restricted to golf and his chances of surviving four of the most difficult and testing competitions in the world. For the operative word here is "surviving." Who would have dreamed that twice between July and September of the year of the Grand Slam, that is to say between his winning the U. S. Open and competing in the U. S. Amateur, Jones would escape death by a fraction of a second and the proverbial eyelash.

A more superstitious era would have sworn that the gods were angry at the temerity of this man in challenging them by setting out to accomplish this feat. During a round of golf at Eastlake that summer, they fired two lightning bolts at him and each time scored near-misses. The first one hit where the Jones foursome ought to have been had they continued on, instead of hesitating about what to do under the circumstances of the sudden thunderstorm.

Then as Jones passed by the clubhouse on his way to the locker room, "they" had one more shot and bull's-eyed the clubhouse chimney. Jones' umbrella was smashed, his shirt ripped down to his waist, and there was a six-inch scratch on his shoulder, but he was otherwise unharmed. After the storm he found the spot where he had been littered with masses of brick and mortar, any one of which would have killed him had it struck him on the head.

Next, the Jealous Ones tried a different method. They sent a runaway automobile after him as he was walking toward the Atlanta Athletic Club, where he had a luncheon engagement. Occupied with his thoughts, he did not hear the juggernaut approaching until a voice behind him called, "Look out, mister!"

Jones turned, saw, and reacted with a jump which he himself said would have done Jesse Owens credit. The car passed exactly over the spot from which he had leaped, and crashed into the wall of the clubhouse. But for the lone pedestrian's warning, he would have been crushed to death. After that the gods gave up and he had only to contend with the amateur golfers of the United States and Canada.

Jones alone would be capable of revealing the nerve strain he endured through those four tournaments; tensions ever increasing and multiplying, to the last test—the American Amateur at Merion—in which he took his final thirty-six-hole match from his opponent, Gene Homans, by the overwhelming score of 8 and 7. He does so, in fact, in his splendid book, *Golf Is My Game*, published in 1960, and it is not at all certain that a severe illness suffered in later life was not attributable as the price paid for these strains.

There have been those inclined to laugh at us in that era for the purple prose we often injected into our accounts of Jones' accomplishments. After all, what was there to this game of walking leisurely through manicured country on a sunny, summer's afternoon, pausing occasionally to strike at a ball that wasn't even moving, compared to the eye needed to knock a baseball pitch out of a park, the courage to crash a football line, the speed of reaction and agility to return a fireball tennis service, or the endurance to survive a pounding in the ring and come on to win?

The fact remains that of all sports, golf in one sense is the most taxing in that it calls for absolute self-control. Those adrenalins which in the boxer, ballplayer, or footballer can whip him to a fighting frenzy and produce a sometimes seemingly miraculous, winning performance are of no use whatsoever to the championship golfer. If anything they are a handicap. He wants no part of this kind of chemistry to upset the precarious balance of nerve and muscle. As I wrote once in a column in the long, long ago, golf is a backwards game; a descent from *crescendo fortissimo* to *pianissimo*. Instead of working up to a climactic effort, the booming drive comes first and at each hole for the finale, with every taut nerve screaming and twanging, the player must impart the most delicate impetus to the ball to cause it to roll over an often rough and uneven lawn and pop down a very small mole hole.

In a golf championship, whether he is playing the seventy-two holes of an Open, or the week's competition of the Amateur, the contender must go on doing exactly the same thing at the end that he has done at the beginning—play against the course and hit the ball in a calm, cool, and relaxed manner. Yet, as he nears the final flag, the tensions are entirely different from what they were at the start. In addition to the other competitors breathing down his neck, he is carrying the burden of wrongly played holes and lost strokes.

And, it must be remembered as well, that he is playing the same layout over and over again. Each hole acquires an identifiable personality and a history of triumph or trouble, so that as the player approaches it, he cannot help but be thinking of the mess he made of it the last round. And this mounting strain Jones endured not once, but four times as he battled on toward the completion of the Grand Slam. Let no one underestimate his suffering during that year of near-miraculous accomplishment, or what it took out of him. I do not hesitate to call this the supreme athletic effort of the decade.

But the four major titles in one season was only the climax to a nine-year career which has not been equaled since.

In nine consecutive attempts at the U. S. Open and, remember, always playing against professionals who were hot and edged from continued winter and spring competition, Jones finished first four times and second four times. Two of the latter he lost in playoffs, indicating that he hit the leading score on six occasions, the last four of them in a row. He won three out of four British Open championships in which he competed, and had a fifty-fifty split in his two tries at the British Amateur.

With practically every record set up then wiped off the books by the more skilled and efficient athletes of the present, the question naturally arises whether anyone will ever equal or surpass the accomplishment of Jones.

Like every other game or sport, golf has become improved and refined to the point where it is far more demanding than ever before. Jones won most of his Open championships with scores ranging between 290 and 296, which today will get you a yard or so of crying towel in the locker room and little more. To have a look in at a modern tournament, you must be at least ten strokes under that total, a reflection of the steel-shafted clubs, beefed-up ball and above all, the fierce and continuing cut-throat battle among the professionals for the big money prizes.

I am convinced that the duplication of Jones' feat is slipping farther and farther away due to the primary condition to be fulfilled by one who wants to match it. For to begin with he must be an amateur.

And he must win that first one, the British Amateur, where he will encounter not only the best players in the British Isles, but wind and weather, and rain sometimes fired by the bucketful in his face as he stands trying to address the ball. Jones' problem was made even more difficult by the fact that in those days, after the qualifying rounds, they played eighteen-hole elimination matches morning and afternoon, before the thirty-six-hole final. Eighteen holes in championship golf is equivalent to sudden death. If you found yourself one or two down on the back nine, your opponent could halve you out of the tournament in no time. Twice in this tournament Jones was carried to the eighteenth green to win, and once by Cyril Tolley to an extra hole, the nineteenth, so that his narrow escapes and the tensions they set up can be imagined.

Well, if such a player-for-fun comes along and does win the British Amateur, he must thereafter take over the world's best professionals—British, American, Canadian, French, Argentine, or whatever is going, in two tournaments of the most difficult and nerve-racking medal play conceivable.

Since the days of Jones there has been only one non-professional who has captured an Open championship. This was our own Johnny Goodman, who took the U.S. title in 1933, but won nothing else that year. The world itself has changed so greatly, socially and physically, within the last forty years that it is doubtful whether such an amateur as Jones could mature, even though he were to duplicate all Bob's endowed mental and physical genius.

The late Grantland Rice, the most graceful of all sportswriters, put it this way in an article written in 1940: "There is no more chance that golf will give the world another Jones than there is that literature will produce another Shakespeare, sculpture another Phidias, music another Chopin. There is no more probability that the next five hundred years will produce another Bob than there is that two human beings will be born with identical fingerprints."

FPG

The world's greatest amateur versus the world's greatest professional, Bob Jones and Walter Hagen tangle in a match. The party with the field glasses around his neck and carrying a notebook, seen just over Jones' right shoulder, would be the author at work in his day.

When Jones returned home after his Grand Slam, Atlanta, Georgia gave him the same treatment that New York gave Ederle.

And so we old ones proudly nominate Jones as the best of the best and the best of all.

We yield that nobody in our day jumped over a bar set at 7 feet 2½ inches, ran a mile in under four minutes, broke the 60-yard sprint barrier or swam, hurdled, or skied as fast as they do today. But the picture of Robert Tyre Jones, Jr. still hangs over the bar of the Old Codgers' and Beard-Mumblers' Club, unassailed and unassailable. None of us who knew him then or, for that matter, even the present or the next generation of sportswriters, will be around to see him shot down.

CHAPTER **15**

Men with the Golden Pen

This one decade which saw the rise of the athlete to such fame and fortune as had hitherto been undreamed of, was at the same time responsible for the transformation of the sportswriter from a semi-illiterate nobody to a star in his own right sometimes, a person of affluence and even some social standing in the community.

I remember during this period there was a considerable hullabaloo about the secret payroll and which sportswriter was on whose for handouts. And there was a good deal of moralizing upon the ethics of accepting presents from promoters or club owners and Pecksniffian looking down of noses by the "honest" upon those who, because they "took," could be considered crooked or dishonest. I might add that there was no such problem on my paper, simply because our publisher let it be known that anyone who accepted so much as a pocket handkerchief would be fired, and to offset this paid salaries which made it completely unnecessary to augment one's income.

But this was not so prior to that ten years where everything for everyone turned to gold. Entry into the sports department was not the ambition of every reporter or newspaperman. Sportswriting at the turn of the century was ill paid and looked down upon, and its practitioners were expected by the publishers to eke out their meager wage by doing publicity for the owner of the baseball club, or printing puffs in the paper for prize fight managers, or boxing promoters and their stumblebums. It was not the writers who were crooked, but the publishers who permitted this kind of swill to appear on their pages, in order to pinch a few pennies from the sports editor's salary.

The opening up of the sports pages following World War I and the growth of every game and the interest therein, due to the caliber of the champions that appeared upon the scene, changed all this.

From being considered one grade above the office cat, the sportswriter, who often had been as much of a tramp and a lush as the lushes and tramps with whom he associated and about whom he wrote, suddenly became a person of substance with motorcar, a house in the country, and the admiration of his fellow citizens. But more important than this, he became literate, and at the very least two of those who flourished during that time have become, or will become, literature. I refer to my late colleagues, Ring Lardner and Damon Runyon.

And if that era gave rise to the greatest concentration of champions and sports personalities in our history, there was also a similar outpouring of men fit to sing of their deeds. It was my own good fortune to have known and worked with them, and they indeed wielded golden pens.

A recent somewhat pompous book on sportswriting and editing accused the practitioners of our time of addiction not so much to the rum, but the purple ink bottle and the composing of stories so ecstatically flowery that they would never for one moment have gotten by the editor of the copy desk of today. We were undoubtedly guilty of perpetrating sentimental tosh, or overexaggerating what was merely a day's work for two professional teams, but it must be remembered that this was a florid era and called more than occasionally for florid reporting to do it justice.

When suddenly you found yourself confronted with a unique character slapping out sixty home runs in a season, where heretofore eight or nine, or at the most a dozen was considered heavy hitting, the old, placid adjectives simply would no longer do. When a Jack Dempsey battered a Luis Firpo five times to the canvas and then was himself slugged clear out of the ring, to come back and knock that same Firpo kicking in the wildest pier six brawl ever seen in the prize ring, who would have had that much water in his veins to produce the lead: "Heavyweight champion Dempsey knocked out challenger Luis Angel Firpo in one minute and thirty-seven seconds of the second round at the

Polo Grounds last night, before a crowd of 75,000. Dempsey weighed 185 pounds to Firpo's 207 pounds."

Poets were needed to celebrate the miracles we were observing on every hand, and poets indeed were being supplied to fill the demand. Grantland Rice was a poet, and so were Damon Runyon, John Kieran, O. B. Keeler, and W. O. McGeehan. These men wrote like angels of the things they saw and felt and some, in fact most of the best writing in the American press of that age, was found on the sports pages. Here was not only drama but wit and humor and an expansion of the language. Where ordinary words were inadequate to tell the tale, these men made up their own. They bestowed unforgettable sobriquets on teams and individuals, and coined slogans in use to this very day.

It is unfortunate that stories, reports, and sports columns that appear in the daily press are writ upon water and this is sad for American literature. Nothing is quite as ephemeral as yesterday's newspaper. Perhaps several hundred years from now, when the raucous decade about which I have been telling has become no more than a single tick of the metronome of time, someone will go back and rescue some of the pieces written by McGeehan or Westbrook Pegler, Henry McLemore, Bill Corum, or Dan Parker, and then they will have as vivid a picture of our era as Charles Dickens left behind of his.

Three men I have already mentioned who will not be immediately forgotten—Runyon, Lardner, Kieran—had the foresight to write books and stories as well as reporting the sporting scene. These volumes can be fingered down from library shelves, and thus half the battle not to be forgotten is already won. Lardner has assured his place in American literature and, if Damon Runyon is not now fully appreciated, it will take no more than a half century or so before he is rediscovered as literary a find and contributor to Americana as Walt Whitman, Washington Irving, Bret Harte, or Mark Twain.

Runyon, the strange, strange character who for twenty years dominated the American sportswriting scene as the greatest of all, bookwise is known only for his Broadway gangster short stories, published in what the literary critics sneer at as the slick magazines—*Cosmopolitan, The Saturday Evening Post,* and the late

Collier's. Yet, long before these appeared, the young Runyon of
Pueblo and Denver, Colorado, unknown in the East, was writing
and selling verse and short stories to the literary magazines and
eventually these will contribute to his survival. There is no question in my mind as to who was the most accurate and often the
master minnesinger of the Golden Decade. It was Runyon.

But there were others in New York, and at least one in every
other big city, who could strum the lyre too, and did, and these
I recall as my friends and colleagues and also as characters as
well, from those wacky days.

And so, too, will my contemporaries remember their names.
There was tall, grave Harry Salsinger of Detroit; thoroughgoing
Don Maxwell, now editor-in-chief of the Chicago *Tribune;* Arch
Ward and Harvey Woodruff, also from Chicago; bulky Bill Cunningham in Boston; the brilliant Ralph McGill from Atlanta, today
probably the greatest liberal editor and publisher in the country;
red-haired Mark Kelly of Los Angeles; knowledgeable Fred Digby
from New Orleans; owl-like Havey Boyle of Pittsburgh, and cyni-
cal Tom Laird of San Francisco.

New York itself was fairly spangled with stars: Grantland Rice,
McGeehan, Corum, Dan Parker, and Joe Williams were all to be
found on metropolitan newspapers, as were Hype Igoe, Frankie
Graham, Kieran, Jim Dawson, Eddy Neal, Allison Danzig, with
Alan Gould writing for the Associated Press, Hank McLemore for
United Press, and Davis Walsh for International News Service.
These and many others, before the days of radio or television,
functioned as the eyes and ears of the great sports-mad public
who could not get to the events themselves and relied upon the
newspapers to bring them color and the excitement of the battle.

Many of these men were not only experts in their field and
good writers, but also stylists and individualists, whose work
would have been recognized even without their by-lines. And
somehow they seem to have been created specifically for their
jobs—the reporting and interpretation of a new kind of national
entertainment. The proof of this particular pudding lay in the
fact that when, upon occasion, big-name writers were hired to
cover some event expected to be so colossal as to be beyond the

powers of the staff reporters, they were universally terrible and dismal flops.

This was likewise testimony to the insatiable appetite for drama of the reading public of those days and the importance of feeding it. Every so often publishers themselves were overawed by a forthcoming clash between titans. Then, without consulting the sports editor, and usually in collaboration with the syndicate manager, they ordered some famous novelist or literary big-shot celebrated on the book pages of the Sunday *Times*, hauled down from his ivory tower and shipped up to the arena, hoping for a jackpot of golden words.

These poor fellows were not only bewildered by the unfamiliarity of it all, but also terrified by the presence of a telegraph operator with an open key at their elbows, waiting for a lead no sooner had the last of the vanquished gladiators been carted from the field. The veteran had been drilled at this juncture to open up his portable and make it say *something*. It was not always *belles-lettres*, but it was in time for the edition. The "sacred cows," as they were known to the regulars, when confronted with this situation, either choked up or perpetrated some awful banality. Sportswriting had become not only a profession but something of an art.

Our sportswriters were as different from one another as oil and water. Damon Runyon wrote with a rasp, often as though scratching out the words with a file; behind the smooth flow of John Kieran's elegant prose was the quiet humor and vast knowledge of a highly educated observer. The personality of Grantland Rice shone through his columns—that of a sweet, gentle man with something endearingly childlike in him, who passionately loved his work and his world. Even as a sportswriter, Westbrook Pegler was using acid instead of ink. O. B. Keeler brought the same charm and erudition to his golf stories, and particularly those involving his idol Jones, as did his opposite number in London, Bernard Darwin who, every time he sat down to report a golf match, could only produce literature.

If the argot of Damon Runyon's gangsters was sometimes like none anyone ever heard in real life, it did not matter since his short stories were fiction. The ear of Dan Parker actually was impeccable in reproducing the exact talk of that new, rich world of prize fight managers, pugs, jockeys, touts, press agents for six-day bicycle races, ballplayers, and small-time promoters who populated his column. All of their weird dialects and fracturing of the English language were faithfully reproduced.

Ring Lardner had captured not only the speech of ballplayers but their thinking and curious psychology too. His "You Know Me, Al" series which ran in *The Saturday Evening Post,* purporting to be the letters of a bush-leaguer, pinioned the breed perfectly. W. O. McGeehan was a dry, whimsical man with a sense of mischief and an untrammeled imagination which made his daily column a joy to read. Men like Bill Cunningham, Joe Williams, Bill Corum, and Alan Gould had descriptive powers and command of words to suit their field. Henry McLemore was a first-class humorist of the sports pages.

But the sportswriters of that day and age fulfilled yet another function hitherto unknown. They assumed the duties of Cato the Censor. Pegler was a veritable Savonarola. Skullduggery was nothing new in the underworld of sports, but before World War I it was small-time stuff. There were crooked fights, crooked horse races, crooked foot races, but they didn't matter, for only an infinitesimal percentage of the public at large was being bit.

But with the sudden growth of nearly every game into the million-dollar class, larceny began to be practiced on a large scale, and the sports page reporters and columnists constituted themselves as watchdogs as much as they were able and the laws of libel permitted.

At the first, faint whiff of the aroma of hydrogen sulphide arising from any prospective promotion, or even mismatches, they took to their typewriters and yelled. They could not guarantee honesty in every sport, but they certainly made it more difficult for the crooks to operate.

It was the vociferous articulateness of the sportswriters that was responsible for the New York Boxing Commission labeling wrestling matches as "exhibitions" instead of contests. When the shameless buildup of the giant Primo Carnera was under way, newspaper readers the country over knew that it was a swindle because their sportswriters told them so; not in so many words, but nevertheless unmistakably. It was one of them, by the name of Hugh Fullerton, who broke the famous Black Sox scandal of a thrown World Series, just before the beginning of the bright decade. There were ways and means of hinting at a fixed fight, tank job, or splash long before it came off, and boxing writers of the caliber of Runyon, Igoe, and Wilber Wood, as well as Eddy Neal of the Associated Press, did not hesitate to do so. Nobody ever collected for libel.

All of this, it must be remembered, was pioneering. The literate writing, the criticism, the free, untrammeled commentary, the policing, and the daily column were all first during that era and have continued on down to this day, even though it would seem that the interest in sports and characters is not at the same fever heat as was attained after World War I.

While in the main I have lost track of American sportswriting in recent years, I would be the last to suggest that the writers of my day had anything over some of the current crop, and men of the caliber of Red Smith and Jimmy Cannon of New York, Doc Green of Detroit, and Jim Murray of Los Angeles are stars in any league. If those of yesteryear linger more vividly in my memory it is because that was when I was young and they were my colleagues, and in the words of Bob Jones' favorite poem, "Men that were boys when I was a boy . . ."

And how youth must color memory and reminiscence. I am prepared to admit it to the present generation. These must be fine times, too, to follow the athletes and be allowed a free pen.

Perhaps the pastures looked greener to me then because it was all so novel. We were the elite of our newspapers and the envy of every office boy, reporter, rewrite man, and some of the editors as well. Day in, day out we traveled the country over, first class on expense account, from one thrill to another. One week we would be wandering about some lovely park of a golf course in the summer sunshine, following the tournament players; the next sitting in the marquee at Forest Hills, or lazing away an afternoon at the ball yard.

If there was something cooking in San Francisco or Los Angeles, Dallas, Detroit, Atlanta, Boston, or New Orleans, we went there and to Europe as well, for that matter. The purse strings of the publishers were wide open and nothing was too great an expense if we sent back a good story.

In my flying days, when I held a pilot's license, I was encouraged to hire aircraft wherever and whenever I wanted one; to fly myself to the Kentucky Derby or attempt an air coverage of the Gar Wood-Kaye Don speedboat races out of Detroit. At one time I had a Loening Amphibian for the coverage of five major sports events in one day: the finals of the Amateur Golf championship in Boston, the America Cup races off Newport R.I., the Futurity Stakes at Belmont Park, Long Island, the International Polo match at nearby Westbury, and lastly a world's championship prize fight in Astoria at night. My "Daisy-the-Duck," as she was called, could sit down on land or water and was invaluable for getting about. There was no complaint about the cost.

We all possessed a magic wand in the shape of a piece of paper labeled, "W.P.," which stood for "Working Press" (the U. S. Golf Association even provided us with individual gold badges, and at Madison Square Garden, our ringside seats were distinguished with brass name plates). These were "open sesame" to the finest vantage points for observing what was going on, the best seats in the house; looking down from heated press boxes on the fifty-yard line upon the football scene below, or with our noses smack up against the ring canvas at prize fights. Nothing was too good for the pampered Working Press. At World Series the club owners provided a drinking and feasting room for social gatherings after the games; during six-day bike races, steaks and beer were on tap for us where the riders had their meals, at any time of the day or night. When we traveled we had drawing rooms or compartments and stayed at the best hotels. If we did not attain the Croesus class of some of the athletes we wrote about, at least we all lived like millionaires.

Because when in early manhood I was so very conscious of veterans harking back to the heroes of their youth, I was always aware of how time was able to fade the colors from the most vivid of portraits, and even then I wondered how the heroes of that day would be able to stand the test. And now, looking backward, I find them unaltered even though times are so changed.

They stand out not alone for their abilities, but their personalities and their stories. All of them in one way or another were involved in high drama. Those who followed seem to be little more than somewhat pallid imitations. I never heard of a heavyweight prize fighting champion of the world being a bore, but the current holder of this title, Cassius Clay, has managed to achieve this as did the chap who succeeded under slightly different circumstances to hit more home runs than Babe Ruth. Even though I have been occupied with other pursuits since 1936, my affection for sports has never flagged, and in recent years I have kept fairly up to date in the goings on, via the Paris *Herald Tribune* and *Time* magazine. I must confess that I have come across very few personalities who genuinely engaged my interest and who made me wish I might see them in action, or be back at the sports desk writing about them.

One of those who did for a moment was Sonny Liston, because he was so utterly monstrous, surly, and bad-tempered, and for a little it looked as though once more we had a real character upon the scene about whom some drama might develop, that is until this snarling panther became a kitten in his corner and meekly quit to one such as Clay. It seemed to me that in our times even quitters quit big.

But there I go again about "our times." They are over and done with, never to return. The present generation will soon be looking upon them as something utterly foreign in speech, dress, custom, and approach to life as then we looked back to the days of the Regency Dandies, or the war between the states, or even that era when Napoleon terrified Europe (when my father was born, there were still veterans of Napoleon's army alive), and wondered what those people really were like and thought and felt.

Recently we celebrated the fiftieth anniversary of World War I, and the soldiers of that time look as different from ours of today as Pershing's boys differed from the men in blue and gray, or one of the Duke of Wellington's Grenadiers. Our clothes, too, have changed, and when I thumb through some of the photographs of myself taken during the 1920s, I see a stranger.

A stranger, I should say, in every way, for I am most certainly no longer the person I was then, nor ever could be again. If I went back to sportswriting I am sure the columns I would do now would be quite different from those of yesteryear, for one reason simply that I should not like to have them laughed at by my readers of today for their innocence, credulity, and overenthusiasm. I don't mind having thus changed, for I am so fortunate as not to live in the past, but thoroughly enjoy the present with all its novelties. I do not particularly want to orbit the earth, or fly to the moon, trussed up in a space capsule, but that is only one of the symptoms of aging. I am still vastly excited by those who do and the boundless horizons which are being opened to man. When I was young I wanted to learn to fly and did, and at that time this was considered about the limit of man's capacity to escape from his planet.

Then why this book? For one reason, because I found enjoyment in writing about my old friends and heroes, and many who were young when they were, and loved them too, and lived a portion of their lives vicariously, might find pleasure in reading about them.

If for nothing else, the present generation of sportswriters should be grateful to me for this volume, for setting up a target. "One more old fogy maundering about the good old days! What about our great champion Whosis? And that fantastic character Whatsis? And the notable So-and-Sos? A sitting duck, this guy!"

To your typewriters, gentlemen!

Saint Bambino

I don't say you should believe this story.

Maybe the whole thing is just the imaginings of an old man who ain't got much more time left to sit in the sun in the grandstand behind third base and listen to that sweet sound when the ash is applied to the middle of the old horse-hide and you know the apple is heading for Railroad Avenue the other side of the fence.

Could be I just dreamed it all, or maybe it was Jimmy Jr.'s dream that I got into somehow. But I know I seen and talked with a real saint.

I seen him just as plain as you're looking at this page, that night a year ago when I went into Jimmy Jr.'s room feeling licked and lower than a snake's piazza because I wasn't getting anywhere with what Jimmy's mother asked me to come to New York for and live with them, which was to try to make a man out of him. You see, the kid didn't care about baseball. That was a terrible thing. Twelve years old and he don't know Mickey Mantle's or Ralph Kiner's batting average, and can't tell you who's leading the league in R.B.I.s.

How bad it is, he don't even know or care who's topping the League, American or National. His teacher in school said he was a natural pull hitter and could make the team if he cared. But all the kid wanted to do was read about space rockets and trips to Mars, and look at Captain Universe on television.

What made it worse is who his father was. And his grandfather. That's me, Harry Murphy.

So this night I am going to tell you about, I'd come back from

a night game at Yankee Stadium, which was just across the way
from where Janet, Jimmy Jr.'s mother, had her flat on Edgecomb
Avenue, and I couldn't sleep. Vic Raschi beats the Detroits 6 to 5
and Mantle hits one in the clutch; I sat alone back of third base.
Used to be a time when I'd dreamed of sitting there with my
grandson. But the kid wasn't having any. He stayed behind to
look at a television show. And it wasn't baseball.

That Yankee Stadium was like home to me. I let out a couple
of blasts at the Yanks, but it wasn't the same like the old days
when the Babe and Lou Gehrig was there and everybody knew
me.

I lay there thinking about what the kid was missing, and what
I could do about it. Maybe I did ask for help. You wouldn't want
to see any boy of yours grow up without caring how the home
team made out, would you? Why, sometimes that's all that holds
the country together when things gets tough.

The next thing I know, it's two o'clock in the morning and I
thought I heard a noise in Jimmy Jr.'s room next door. So I got
up to look, thinking maybe he wasn't well or wanted something.

But when I came in, I could see he was sleeping peacefully,
for there was a moon over Coogan's bluff lighting up the Polo
Grounds on the other side of the river, and it came in the window.
Then I saw the stranger sitting by his bedside.

He was a great big guy built like a beer barrel. I should of
jumped a mile high from scare, but right away I saw there was
something familiar about him. He was wearing a big camel's-
hair polo coat with a belt, and a tan camel's-hair cap. His head
was turned and he was looking down at Jimmy Jr., but when I
came into the room he switched around so that the moon lit up
his face and I saw who it was. I'd of known that big ugly mug
with the little piggy eyes and the nose spread all over his face
anywhere in the world.

And at that moment I didn't even stop to think that he'd been
dead five years. I said, "Hello, Babe!"

He said, "Hello, keed. How's things?" but didn't get up or offer
to shake hands. He just sat there, his jaws moving on a big plug
of tobacco he had in his mouth.

I couldn't think of anything to say but, "The Yanks won to-night, 6 to 5. Mantle got hold of one in the eighth."

He nodded. "Yeah, I know. I was there. That's a good kid that Mantle, but he ought to stick to one side or the other. Them switch hitters ain't never consistent."

"Boy," I said: "Babe Ruth. Am I glad to see you!" All of a sudden it came home to me who I was talking to. "Hey," I whispered so as not to wake Jimmy Jr., "what's going on? You're dead, aren't you?"

The Babe grunted. "Uhuh! Deader than Kelcey."

"Then what are you doing here?"

The Babe chewed on his plug for a while before replying, "You sent for me, didn't you?"

"Me?" I was so mixed up by this time I couldn't remember who I was talking to.

"I dunno," the Babe said, "You oughta know what's cooking. We got a call about a half-hour ago. The manager told me to get my pants off the bench and take a look in here."

It came back then, what I'd been doing a half-hour ago. I ain't much of a religious man, but when it comes down to it and a member of my family is in trouble like Jimmy Jr. was, I ain't ashamed to pray.

I said, "I remember now. I asked the saints to help me."

"Okay," the Babe said. "What's on your mind, keed?"

Much as I loved the big monkey, I couldn't help letting out a snort. "Hey! What are you giving me? You a saint?"

The Babe for a second actually managed to look modest, which was never one of his long points, though maybe sheepish was a better way to describe it, and he said hastily, "I know, I know. I done all kinds of fat-headed things when I was around here, didn't I? Women, liquor, horsing around. . . . But *they* got a way of overlooking those, if you say you're sorry when you get *there*, or if you were too dumb to know what you were doing. So after I'd been there a couple of years and kept my nose clean, *they* made me a saint."

I couldn't figure it out. In my book, the Babe was the greatest man that ever lived, but they got rules for that sort of thing. I said, "I thought you had to be made a saint from down here."

The Babe's ugly puss busted into a big grin. He replied, "Up there they don't always wait. Particularly when they got use for a guy."

I asked, "How did it happen, Babe?"

He chawed a while and then replied, "I dunno. One day one of them came along and says, 'Hey, Babe. What about that time you got up at that dinner to Jimmy Walker and promised to turn over a new leaf for the sake of the dirty-faced kids in the street?' I says, 'What about it?' He says, 'Were you on the level? Did you really mean it?' I says, 'What do *you* think? Ain't you never seen a kid with his heart broke because something or somebody he believed in went sour?' He says, 'Okay, Babe. That's all I wanted to know. You come along with me. We got work for you to do.' So they put me on the roster."

I said, "Well, what do you know? What are you saint of? What do I call you?"

He shifted his chew and said affably, "Call me Babe. Up there I'm known as Saint Bambino, but I don't go much for that stuff. Baseball, of course. It's the biggest thing in the world, ain't it?"

I started to say, "You're tellin' me . . ." when he continued.

"There's millions of kids in this country to whom baseball's mighty important. They worry, and snivel themselves to sleep because they can't hit a curve ball, stop pulling back from a fast one inside, or hold a hot liner with the meat hand. Or maybe they're weak on grounders hit to the left of them, or don't like to block the bag at second when a bigger guy is trying to steal or stretch a single. Sometime's it's a matter of timing. Others, it's moxie. I'm in charge of that."

"Yeah, is that right? What do you do?"

Babe turned to the window and let go some tobacco juice.

He said, "Oh, I dunno. Take a look around and maybe ask Number One, the manager, to give 'em a hand. Unless they ask for me personally, like some do. . . ." He grinned again. "There was that kid last week in Biloxi, Mississippi. He threw wild to home plate from left field, let two runs in, and lost the game. All the other kids picked on him. That night he asked me if I'd ever pulled one like that? He kept bellerin', 'Babe, I bet you never did that. Babe, I'm no good. I wanna die. Help me. . . .'"

"So what did you do?"

"So I reminded the kid about that time in Cleveland in 1925 when we were two games out of first place for the pennant the last week in August."

I said, "What happened? I don't remember that one."

The Babe laughed that big old deep rumbling laugh of his. "We're leading 6–5 in the last of the ninth. The Indians got two on and two out. What's-his-name, their shortstop, comes up and I figured him for a short single between first and second if he hits, and come in to take it on the first hop."

"And does he?"

"Sure. And I got the runner for home out by a mile, only I'm still full of beer from the night before and throw the ball right over the top of the Press box. Boy, Hug was sore. He slapped a hundred-dollar plaster on me. I told him to keep his shirt on, I'd get the game back for him."

"And did you?"

"Sure . . . I got hold of two the next day. Day after that I clobbered 'em. I got a single, a double, and two triples, and threw Whosis, their second baseman, out at the plate with the tying run from the right-field fence. Hug took the plaster off."

"What about the kid from Biloxi?"

"He quit blubberin'. He'll go out and try to win the next three games and make 'em forget his error. Remember how they used to razz me when I struck out? They'd forget all the strike-outs when I got the wood onto one."

I moved so that the light from the moon through the window fell onto my face. The Babe suddenly took a good gander at me.

"Say," he said, "I seen you before some place. Hey, wait a minute! Ain't you that red-faced turkey used to sit back of the boxes behind third base in the stadium and ride me all the time in the old days? I can't remember the name. . . ."

Babe never could remember anybody's name, not even the guys on his own team. But I could of busted with pride and almost cried to think he knew me.

"Murphy," I said, "Leather Lung Murphy!"

The Babe slapped his knee. "That's the son-of-a-sailor," he said. "Boy, that brass voice of yours used to get under my skin."

How it all came back to me then, those years when I used to give it to him back in the old days. The Babe would come up to bat, and I'd holler, "Strike out, ya bum! Oh, what a bum!" And if he'd hit one I'd bawl, "Oh, you lucky stiff!"

They said my voice would carry all the way down to the 138th Street Harlem River bridge. The crowd would whoop and holler and laugh and turn around and point me out, saying, "That's Leather Lung Murphy from Detroit. He always rides the Babe." The papers wrote pieces about me and the kids would come up and ask for my autograph. I was as famous as any of 'em.

It was like I could close my eyes and be back there more than twenty-five years ago and see Yankee Stadium on a summer's afternoon with the Babe up to bat. The outfield seemed greener then, the ball whiter, the uniforms brighter, the crowds bigger and better.

There would be the Babe at the plate. He had a body shaped like a pear and he'd stand up on those thin, pipe-stem ankles of his with the number "3" on his back, leaned over a little, waving his big bat a little. I remember how the elevated trains would slow down as they passed the stadium so the motorman could see whether the Babe got hold of one. Nobody could make any mistake, no matter from how far, who it was up.

He'd have his big paws wrapped around the bat handle so it looked like a matchstick in his fingers. The pitch would come; he'd miss it with an almighty swipe and wrap himself around so his legs was twisted like a pretzel. A roar would go up and on top of it would be me like a brass trumpet yelling, "Strike out, ya bum!"

There'd be another throw and he'd be taking a backswing before the ball got out of the pitcher's grip. Then you'd hear a click—it wasn't a crack, or a bang, or a thud, but a click like no other sound you ever heard; it was never different, and it always meant the ball was out of the park over the right-field fence.

Boy, that roar! And that big ape trotting around the bases on them too-small dogs of his, tipping his cap. And maybe giving me a grin when I handed him the bird as he rounded third base.

Pretty soon the game'd be over, the fans would be streaming across the diamond, I'd go home to a big thick steak my good wife, Ellen, would have cooked for me and tell my Jimmy, who was eight, what his big hero the Babe had done that day. That was the life. It was never so good, before or after.

The Babe shifted in his chair next to Jimmy Jr.'s bed and said, "What was it you had it in for me in them days, Murph?"

"Nothing personal, Babe," I replied, "I come from Detroit, so there was only one ball player in the world for me, Ty Cobb."

It was true. I was born and raised in Detroit. After you'd watched the Georgia Peach play you couldn't see no other diamond jockey for dust. When I come out of the Army in 1919, I stayed in New York and got a job as a mechanic. Afterwards I got into the garage business and made my pile. But I'm always a Tiger rooter because that's how I was born.

Babe was scratching his head like he was trying to think back on something. Finally it come to him.

"What made you quit riding me, Murph? Seemed like one day all of a sudden you wasn't there any more. I missed you, keed. You used to get my goat so I'd want to bust that apple clear out to Hunts Point."

I said, "On the level, don't you remember, Babe?"

He looked at me with surprise. "Naw," he replied. "What happened, keed?"

"Don't you remember little Jimmy Murphy in St. Agatha's Hospital, the kid who was so sick the doctors give him up?"

The Babe still looked blank. Me, I could hardly choke down the lump in my throat. Ever since I come into the room and see him sitting there by Jimmy Jr.'s bedside, I got another scene in my mind just like it, when my boy Jimmy was dying back in 1926. Some sportswriter got wind of it and fixed up a visit from the Babe because my kid was as crazy a fan for Babe Ruth as I was for Ty.

I can still see it like yesterday, the big monkey sitting next to my Jimmy's bed in the hospital. It was God come down from Heaven in a tan polo coat and go-to-hell cap, holding an autographed baseball. He said, "You lissen to the game on the raddio tomorrow, keed. I'm gonna bust one for you." He did, too. I was with Jimmy and seen the glaze go out of his eyes and the color come back to his cheeks. After that, am I going to razz the Babe any more? To me, he's just the greatest man in the world.

"Yeah?" said Saint Bambino. "So what happened?"

I said, "You come to the hospital, autographed a baseball for him, and promised to hit a home run for him."

"Yeah?" said Saint Bambino, "did I? How'd he make out?"

He didn't remember. I suppose he visited a lot of kids in hospitals in his career. There was that Johnny Whosis for whom he hit a home run in the World Series, and a boy in New Jersey, one in Chicago, and another in Boston.

I said, "He got well. But he wouldn't of if it hadn't been for you."

"That's good," Saint Bambino said. "He must be a big guy now. Whatever become of him?"

I swallowed so I would steady my voice. "He was leading a company in the Hurtgen Forest in the last war," I said. "A Heinie threw a potato masher. He covered it with his body to keep his men from being clobbered."

Saint Bambino chewed his wad for a considerable time before he nodded and said, "That's bad."

I nodded toward Jimmy Jr. asleep next to him. "That's his kid there."

The saint looked down at him. I never would have thought such tenderness could spread over that ugly mush. For the first time I noticed a faint glow that seemed to surround or come from the wide-brimmed camel's-hair cap on the big head. "Is it, now?" he said. "What would be his trouble? What made you send for me?"

I had to swallow again hard before I spoke. "Saint," I said finally, "he don't care about baseball."

The Babe chewed and let another stream out the window. When he spoke again it was to say, "That's real bad. How did that happen?"

"After his father was killed, his mother never remarried," I explained. "Women don't understand about baseball like men. The kid's father was the greatest Yankee fan in the world, but Jimmy Jr. grew up without a man around the house. All he wants to do is look at television shows and read space comics."

"That's terrible," Saint Bambino said. "Comics is okay if a game is rained out and you got nuthin' else to do . . ."

"A year or so ago, his mother smarted up to what was going on," I continued. "The boy was pale and didn't eat good. He shoulda been out with the other kids running the bases beltin' that apple and have his head full of something worth while instead of them bum television jokes. I was back in Detroit where I had a string of garages. When the good wife, Ellen, died six months ago I sold out and retired. Janet—that's Jimmy Jr.'s mother—telephoned me to come here and live with them and work on the boy. But it's too late. He just don't care."

So we sat there a minute, looking down at Jimmy Jr. He was a good-put-together kid with his mother's mouth and his father's fighting chin, but he was thin and his color wasn't right.

Saint Bambino leaned forward a little in his chair and began to talk in a low, deep voice. Only he wasn't talking to me any longer, but to the kid.

"Jimmy Jr., lissen to me," he said. "Don't you make no mistake. Baseball's the greatest game in the world, and any man can be proud to have a connection with it no matter what, even if it's only sitting in the grandstand and keeping a box score and yelling for the home team to git out and get them runs."

I thought Jimmy Jr. would wake up, but he don't. He just moved a little in his sleep.

"Do you know what baseball can do, Jimmy Jr.?" the saint continued. "It can take a nobody out of the gutter, maybe somebody that's seen the inside of a jail or a reform school, and make him a bigger man than the President of the United States. Now, you tell me any other game that can do that and I'll kiss your fist."

The moon was starting to slide past the open window now and it seemed like the glow coming from the camel's-hair cap on the big dark head was brighter.

"Don't kid yourself, Jimmy Jr.," the saint went on. "You gotta be a man to play baseball. It's the roughest game in the world, because you gotta have everything. You gotta have condition, co-ordination, speed, science, know-how, hustle, and moxie. Plenty of moxie, son, because if you ever show a yellow streak, the pitchers'll dust you, the base runners'll cut you to ribbons, and the bench jockey's will ride you right out of the league.

"You can't let up for a minute, keed. You got to give it every-thing you got and use the old bean besides. You let one get by you in April, and maybe you find out it's the error that's cost you the pennant in September. You can't slack off, or ease up. When you're in there at bat, or running the bases, you got nine guys working against you, and a big brain sitting on the bench as well, figuring out how to make a monkey out of you."

I never heard such earnestness in any man's voice as in the saint's. He leaned a little further forward and went on.

"Keed, there never was a game figured out prettier to test a man for speed and guts and the old whip; whether the runner gets to the bag first or the ball beats him. Ninety feet between bases, and guys like Ty Cobb was fast enough to steal home, while the pitcher is winding up and letting it go. Sixty feet from the pitcher's mound to home plate and you got maybe a half a second while the ball is in the air to pick out whether you're going to be a hero or a bum. It takes real men to put together a double play and make it look easy and graceful-like."

"Why do you suppose so many millions of people, grown-up men and women as well as kids, Jimmy Jr., love baseball? Why, for so many reasons I could sit here all night long and tell ya. Some of the finest men that ever breathed the air of our country has been in baseball, men everybody can look up to and be proud of because they never give anything but the best they had.

"It's a game, and yet it's like life, keed, and it gets you ready for it. Maybe the score is 10 to 0 against you in the ninth with two out. Half the crowd is heading for the exits because they figure you ain't got a chance. But *you* know you ain't dead un-til there's three out, so you go up there to the plate and take your cut and next thing you know the pitcher is walking to the showers, the new one ain't warmed up good, and you clobber him; the fans stop walking out and five minutes later you got the game in the bag. Nobody ever played baseball, keed, or fol-lowed them that did that wasn't the better for it."

His voice dropped even lower, until it was just like a deep, soft, friendly growl. "It's a team game, Jimmy, and it's ours. It come out of the guts of this country. That's why we're so hard to lick when the chips are down, because when we get into a jam, we play it like a team instead of every man for hisself. A soldier or a sailor or an airman will back up his buddy because maybe he's learned somewhere on some sandlot, or inside a stadium that a pitcher can throw his heart out, but you gotta spear those liners and pick those drives off the fences and then go out and get him some runs, or it don't do no good. It's like you're a family, or a lot of brothers working together. Even if you just sit in the stands and watch you can feel the good in it and learn the lessons that are gonna help you some time when you're in need."

The saint paused for a moment, then gently patted Jimmy Jr. on the thin shoulder that was sticking out from under the sheet.

"That's all for now, keed," he said. "Think it over. Good luck. I may be seeing you again some time . . ." I thought that Jimmy Jr. seemed to smile in his sleep. The saint turned to me. "Okay, Murph. I guess I won't be needed around here any longer so I'll be beating it. The kid'll be okay. If you ever need me again, holler. I'll be keeping an eye on him."

I was all choked up, but I managed to say, "Is there anything I can do for you, Babe—I mean Saint Bambino? . . ."

He thought for a moment, and then got up from the chair. The moon was gone, but from the glow on his cap I could see a kind of sheepish grin on his big mug.

"Yeah," he said, "maybe there is. Things are kind of quiet-like where I am. Just for old time's sake, gimme the old razz, I'd like to hear the old leather lung just once more."

"Which one?" I asked. "I hate to do it to you, Babe."

He grinned again. "The strike-out one. It used to keep me on my toes."

I saw he was on the level, so I let him have it just like I used to with all the brass and steam I had left . . .

"Strike out, ya bum!"

For a moment I thought I could hear the roar of the crowd again, and the sharp "CLICK" that meant the management was out another baseball.

Jimmy Jr. woke up with a start, but when he saw me he quieted right down. "Oh, Granddad," he said. . . . . "Was that you? I was having a dream about Babe Ruth and baseball. . . ."

I started to say that the Babe, or rather Saint Bambino, was right there, but when I looked to where he had been he was gone. Instead, Jimmy Jr.'s mother came hustling into the room in her dressing gown, saying:

"Land's sakes! What's happened, Dad, you yelling fit to wake the dead?"

I said, "I was only showing Jimmy Jr. how I used to holler at the Babe in the old days."

"At this time of morning when the child ought to be getting some rest. I declare, you men. . . ."

But Jimmy Jr. just lay there looking up at the ceiling. After a little he said, "That was a funny dream, but I liked it. Granddad, can I go to the ball game with you tomorrow?"

Yeah, there's one more part to the story, and you don't got to believe that, either.

Last week Jimmy's school nine is playing in the crucial game with Jimmy Jr. catching and batting in the clean-up position. It's two out in the ninth, Jimmy is up. The bases are loaded and we need those runs. In a couple of seconds the pitcher, a big, tough kid with a nasty eye, has breezed two strikes past my Jimmy Jr., and one of 'em is a duster that almost took the P.S.A.L. lettering off his chest. Two and none, and I can see the boy is shaken by the duster. We're in a bad hole.

All of a sudden I hear a familiar voice say, "Move over, keed." I look up, and it's the big guy in the tan polo coat and go-to-hell cap. He sits down next to me.

"Babe," I said, "you got here just in time. The kid's in a spot. . . ."

The saint laughs his deep rumbling laugh. "Take it easy, keed," he says, "just you watch him."

I look. And there's Jimmy Jr., standing at the plate, his bat over one shoulder, and with his free hand he's pointing out to the center-field fence just like the Babe did that day in the World Series in Chicago. It rattles the tough kid just enough. He lets the pitch go. SMACK!

No, it wasn't a homer, but for what was needed, just as good, a triple to deep center that clears the bases.

The saint laughs again, deeper and more satisfied. "The old trade mark," he says, and grins out to where Jimmy Jr. is roosting on third base. "That's the keed. Didn't get enough of the old back porch into that one. A little more meat on your piazza and it's over the fence. Gotta work on them wrists of yours, too. Ain't quite cocking them enough on the backswing. Well, so long, keed . . ."

I heard that big laugh again as he vanished, and then it was lost in the noise of the crowd cheering for Jimmy Jr.